CAMOUFLAGE

CAMOUFLAGE

A History of Concealment and Deception in War

Guy Hartcup

Pen & Sword
MILITARY

On account of *Remus*, a Border collie,
evading deer in Richmond Park, the idea
for this book first took shape

———————————

First published in United States of America in 1979 by David & Charles Inc
Reprinted in this format in 2008
PEN & SWORD MILITARY
an imprint of
Pen & Sword Books Ltd
47 Church Street
Barnsley
South Yorkshire
S70 2AS

ISBN 978 1 84415 769 3

A CIP catalogue record for this book is
available from the British Library

Printed and bound in Great Britain
By Biddles

Pen & Sword Books Ltd incorporates the imprints of
Pen & Sword Aviation, Pen & Sword Maritime, Pen & Sword Military,
Wharncliffe Local History, Pen & Sword Select,
Pen & Sword Military Classics and Leo Cooper.

For a complete list of Pen & Sword titles please contact
PEN & SWORD BOOKS LIMITED
47 Church Street, Barnsley, South Yorkshire, S70 2AS, England
E-mail: enquiries@pen-and-sword.co.uk
Website: www.pen-and-sword.co.uk

CONTENTS

INTRODUCTION

'As I did stand my watch upon the hill
I looked towards Birnam, and anon, methought,
The wood began to move.'
                              Messenger to Macbeth

If an optician were to bring me a similar piece of optical
apparatus [the human eye] I would immediately send it back.
                              Herman Helmholtz

Man has practised the art of concealment and deception in hunting
and warfare from the earliest times. Around 15000 BC a figure called
'The Sorcerer', since its discovery in the twentieth century AD, was
painted on the walls of a cave known as Les Trois Frères in the Ariège
Valley north of the Pyrenees. He wears the skin of a reindeer with
antlers attached to his head. Whether the artist's intention was to
depict a hunter disguising himself as his prey, or whether the animal's
skin conferred supernatural powers on the wearer, we do not know.
In support of the theory of 'magic' it will be shown that on certain
occasions in war disruptive painting on a factory was believed by the
workers to provide immunity from air attack; while some crews of
merchant ships which were dazzle-painted believed that this in itself
guaranteed immunity from submarine attack.

This is a history of *visual* camouflage as practised from the earliest
times to the present day. The word first came into use in World War I
and derived from the French verb *camoufler*, 'to make up for the
stage', though it has antecedents dating from the sixteenth century
via the word *camouflet*, a practical joke. Brown paper was twisted
into a conical shape; its lower edge was lit and its apex held under
the nose of the unsuspecting victim asleep in a chair. He was abruptly
awakened by the smoke filling his nostrils. As a more deadly form of
practical joke, 'camouflet' became a term in military engineering
describing a small mine used as a countermeasure against the enemy's
tunnelling operations.

In a general sense, camouflage is the art of concealing the fact that
you are concealing. But from the military point of view it is more
complex and is best defined under the headings concealment, deception or misdirection, and screening.

There are two aspects of concealment: first there is the sense in
which factories, airfields, installations, ships, aircraft, and troops and
their equipment merge into the background making use of natural
and artificial means such as paint or materials. Characteristic examples

were the disruptive patterns painted on the roofs and sides of aircraft factories to confuse the aerial bomb-aimer and the covering of artillery with netting as concealment against the airborne camera. Second, there is the disguise of an especially vulnerable warlike object or target to make its appearance different and therefore uninteresting to the enemy. The covering of a distinctive sheet of water such as the Maesche Lake near Hannover, which was used as a navigational aim by Allied bombers, or the erection of an additional funnel on a tanker to deceive the U-boat commander, are examples.

Deception or misdirection may be divided, first into general attempts to mislead the enemy as to intention, to give a false idea of strength, or to draw the enemy's attention away from a real attack. An outstanding example was the deception scheme before the British attack at El Alamein so that a false axis of attack was indicated by means of dummy vehicles, tanks and dumps, while the real offensive was prepared in great secrecy elsewhere. In naval warfare confusion in the mind of the attacker is usually achieved by disruptive patterns of paint. Second, methods of local deception such as attempts to distract attention from a real target by means of decoys or to make the enemy expend his strength and ammunition on a false target. Decoy fires outside British towns and industrial targets helped misdirect the bombs of the enemy's main force who believed they were dropping their loads on the flares of their pathfinders. The siting of dummy artillery or tanks are examples of the latter.

Screening includes the concealed screen, which may take the form of false crests, walls, or hedgerows, or visible screens intended to hide military activity or act as a decoy. The screening of roads from ground observers in the vicinity of the front line was frequently practised in World War I and occasionally in the second. Smoke, of course, frequently hides movement or misleads the enemy.

Deception also includes the transmission of false information by radio and other means, the planting of false operation orders, orders of battle and other *ruses de guerre*. Their purpose is to mislead the intelligence service of the enemy about the strength of the forces opposing him or future plans of attack. These aspects of deception in the main fall outside the province of this book.

Camouflage varies according to whether the object will be viewed from the air or the ground and also the climate, terrain and the type of warfare. Mobile operations usually demand no more than the use of local vegetation assisted by nets but static warfare, in the case of camouflage of industrial targets against air attack, has required physicists, engineers, chemists and architects because of their knowledge of structures and materials. At sea, scientists with a knowledge of optics and physiologists are the most likely to solve problems where atmosphere and light affect visibility. However, the artist, with his understanding of the subtleties of colour, tone and texture and his ability to draw on visual memory, has probably contributed the most to military camouflage in all its forms.

Photography from satellite infra-red and thermal cameras, illumination by laser beams, and radar have all demanded a more scientific examination of camouflage materials. In conclusion, therefore, we will look at present methods of camouflage.

Hunters and trappers have matched their cunning against animals which adapt themselves to their surroundings, but study of the principles of camouflage in nature is relatively new. Three men, in particular, have drawn attention to the importance of basing military camouflage on the principles found in nature. First was the American painter/naturalist, Abbott H. Thayer, who died in 1921. His book *Concealing Coloration in the Animal Kingdom* was published five years before World War I and undoubtedly influenced the widespread development of colour camouflage that war stimulated. Second, there was John (later Sir John) Graham Kerr, a Scottish zoologist, who as a young man took part in several expeditions to the Gran Chaco in South America. Not only studying nature, but also hunting animals for food made him appreciate the effectiveness of animal camouflage. Vivid memories of deer suddenly bursting into life in front of him, the ghostly figure of a jaguar bounding in a jungle clearing, or an apparent ant hill resolving itself into a squatting rhea, were recalled some years later when he saw the German and French fleets painted in a uniform obliterative grey at the opening of the Kiel Canal, while the British ships still wore their black paint and yellow funnels. Third, one of his pupils, Hugh Cott, who became Director of Zoology at Cambridge, in 1940 published his classic *Adaptive Coloration in Animals*, which contains frequent references to the military applications of his theme. He expounded his ideas as an instructor in the Middle East and elsewhere.

While it would be misleading to press an analogy between instinctive camouflage in nature and the requirements for camouflage in war, nature's use of camouflage is, by and large, for the same purpose.[1] Survival in nature, as scientists from Darwin to the present have made us aware, depends on food and safety. Survival is a struggle : speed, surprise and, above all, concealment are essential.

Recognition of any object, animate or inanimate, must depend on how form is affected by differences in colour or tone and changes in light and shade. Animals make use of one or more of these factors in the following ways. First, and most obvious, is *colour resemblance* to the environment in which the creature lives. So the ptarmigan nests on the lichen-covered rock of a mountain summit, or the bittern stands motionless in the reeds. More interesting is the way totally unrelated groups in the animal world adopt the characteristic colours of an area.

Predominant colours in desert, for example, are ochre, buff, brown and sandy grey. These colours are reflected not only in the fur of the jackal or the jerboa, the feathers of the great bustard, sand grouse, or quail, but also, on a smaller scale, in the desert lizard, the horned toad and the horned viper. Still more remarkable is the reaction of animals to changes in the colour of terrain within a relatively small area. Lizards may be almost white against light-coloured sand, but nearly black in an area covered with lava; butterflies are known to change colour in a remarkably short time when moved from a rural to an urban area.

The second way to achieve inconspicuousness is by *shading or countershading* (lightening), so destroying the appearance of round-ness or relief resulting from light or shade. It was to countershading that Abbott Thayer was concerned to draw his fellow naturalists' attention. The zebra is a subtle example of countershading. It is almost invisible at dusk and dawn, the times when it is most vulner-able. The dark stripes break the contour lines of its body. On the lower parts, which tend to be shaded and rather darker in colour, the stripes are narrower while on the upper lighted parts the stripes are broad. Thus, instead of being made solid by natural shadows, the body appears flat. Countershading is also found in the jaguar's spots or the patterns on the ocelot, innumerable birds, snakes, lizards and fish. The tunny and the mackerel are dark on the upper surface and light underneath—reflecting their life roles as both pursuer and pursued. Animals also develop structural camouflage to eliminate shadows: tree geckos have flap-like outgrowths and cuttle fish emit a protective screen.

Thirdly, animals are concealed by *disruptive patterning*. Patches of colour draw the observer's attention away from the underlying form of the animal, enabling it to blend with its environment. Obvious examples are ringed plovers and woodcocks against their respective backgrounds of pebbles or woodland. More spectacular are the toads of South America, dull or earth-coloured in appearance but having a vivid yellow stripe running from the nose along the back. This device breaks up the form of the toad, making it look like two half toads so as to confuse an enemy. Patterns may not only disrupt but also join up disparate parts of the body. There is the example of the East African tree frog, which has broad and conspicuous shapes on its back coincid-ing with similar shapes on its hindlegs—an effect rather like a dazzle-painted ship.

Deception, as opposed to concealment, is also practised in nature and used to distract attention from a vital part of the body. Dummy eyes appear on the wing margins of many butterflies or in the sacral regions of certain frogs. Mimicry is another form of deception: the animal looks like something else—a leaf (the swinging mantis), a twig, or a flower (a flower-like moth waits in a bush for its insect prey).

In support of the theory of protective colouring, naturalists are agreed that well-camouflaged animals are noticed and eaten less often than non-camouflaged ones under the same conditions. Total protection, however, through camouflage or deception is no more possible to achieve than it is in warfare.

Man's knowledge of concealment and deception is derived from his need to hunt and trap. The skills he acquired were later transferred to warfare. There are few recorded examples in early warfare. The story of the Trojan horse springs to mind but, less well known, it is believed that during the siege of Syracuse in 212 BC the Greek defenders constructed a false beach covered with straw and supported by a light structure. The first wave of the Roman assault force was deceived by the smooth slope and the Greeks fell on them as they floundered towards dry land.

A similar trap was employed by Robert Bruce against the English at the battle of Bannockburn in 1314. Bruce's troops dug pits and lined them with stakes (a ruse familiar to many primitive tribes). They next sowed the ground with caltrops to spike the feet of the English horses. Bruce stationed his own cavalry in nearby thickets from which they would fall upon the confused English. Bruce also instructed his camp followers to display themselves ostentatiously on the brow of a hill in order to give an impression of false strength.

The use of dummies in warfare also has a long history. The turning point of the Venetians' attack on the city of Ragusa in 1171 came after they set up a fort of cardboard in a dominating position to threaten the defenders. In 1513 the Flemish defenders of Tournai painted and set up lengths of canvas which resembled fortifications in order to deceive the English troops of the extent of the defences. Dummy artillery has frequently been employed.[2]

Deception has also been practised in naval warfare. During the mutiny of the Nore in 1797 it was imperative for the British navy, then blockading French ports, to maintain the impression that a force was still operating at sea. Two or three ships were sent across the Channel manned by loyal seamen. As they appeared over the horizon, they gave bogus signals to non-existent ships so that the enemy assumed more vessels were following them.

The need to make soldiers less visible has been a more recent development. In the nineteenth century the range of weapons increased dramatically. At the close of the Napoleonic Wars the smooth-bore muzzle-loaders carried by infantry were accurate only up to 220yd. Forty years later rifled barrels had come into use and those carried in the Crimean War were accurate up to 1,300yd. Armies had now to discard their distinctive uniforms, adopt more open formations, and merge into the landscape in which they were operating. The colour of a uniform is, of course, only effective at a distance. At closer ranges, form and movement are more important than colour.

The first troops to wear khaki were the Indian Guides, a para-military force raised by Col Sir Harry Lumsden in 1846.[3] They copied the fashion in the local bazaar and dyed their white clothing a mud colour (khaki is the Urdu for dust). Lumsden was sufficiently impressed by their appearance to have khaki-coloured cloth manu-factured in England and sent out to India. The Guides' adoption of khaki, far from giving them cover nearly brought about their destruc-tion when, in 1849, they went into action with British troops for the first time. A section of Guides, racing up a hillside ahead of other units, was taken for the enemy by a British gunner officer. He was about to give the order to fire when one of his men called out, 'Lord, Sir, them is our mudlarks!'

During the Afghan War in 1880 British troops dyed their white summer drill tunics a sort of khaki by boiling them with tea leaves, and during the cold season wore khaki over red serge. This fashion was copied by other British troops in India, though whether for concealment or comfort it is hard to say. The practice spread and in the Egyptian War of 1881–2 the British Army wore khaki, except for their white pith helmets which were stained with tea leaves. 'It was', wrote the future Lt-Gen Sir John Grierson, about the night march to Tel-el-Kebir, 'a most weird sight to see all the troops in khaki and almost invisible marching along the canal bank.'

At the turn of the century three technical developments had a radical effect on warfare. They were: the general adoption of the small-bore magazine rifle, which fired smokeless powder and could hit targets at ranges over 2,000yd; the introduction of the machine gun firing 300 rounds a minute; and quick-firing artillery. According to Maj-Gen J. F. C. Fuller:

> Due to smokeless powder the old terror of a visible foe had given way to the paralysing sensation of advancing on an invisible one. A universal terror, rather than a localised danger, now enveloped the attacker, while the defender, always ready to protect himself by some rough earth- or stone work, was enabled because of the rapidity of rifle fire, to use extensions unheard of in former battles, and in consequence overlap every frontal infantry attack.[4]

These lessons were painfully learned by the British in the Boer War. After it, the wearing of khaki was extended to home service. Although there were experiments with a sort of field grey, khaki serge became a general issue in 1902, probably because it was believed fighting in a European theatre was unlikely. The drab colour was adopted after trials for visibility. The documents containing the criteria governing these trials were unfortunately destroyed, but it seems unlikely they were scientifically reasoned.[5] Otherwise the British Expeditionary Force would not have been sent to fight in 1914 wearing stiff round caps, obvious by their silhouette and the shine from the flat tops.

Not unlike the British, the Japanese in the war with Russia in 1905 wore a yellow-green uniform, harmonising with the Manchurian landscape and the infantry advanced in open order to present a less concentrated target. Continental armies were also discarding uniforms more appropriate for ceremonial purposes and donning clothing which merged into the heaths, rolling grey-green plains and woodland of eastern France and Germany. Field grey was a suitable colour for these regions and was adopted by the German Army in 1910 after trials had taken place with earth-coloured tunics for night operations two years earlier. But the retention by the infantry of their spiked helmets and by the Uhlan Lancers of the distinctive *czapka* rather detracted from these attempts at obscurity. After toying with the possibility of mignonette green, the French adopted horizon blue after World War I had begun, though some units entered the struggle wearing red trousers.

At sea new weapons demanded that more attention be paid to making ships less conspicuous. During the American Civil War of 1861–5, British merchant ships running the Atlantic blockade were painted dull white and their funnels were bent over the upper deck and one side of the vessel so that their own smoke gave cover. Ships thus fitted were believed on occasion to have passed the blockading vessels at a few cables length. In the opening stages of the Spanish–American War of 1898, fought at sea, American warships were painted white, though whether this was done with the intention of reducing visibility is not known. Abbott Thayer took the opportunity of recommending the US Navy Department to study the problem of protective colouring for warships, but his advice seems to have been ignored.

The threat posed by the torpedo and the development of long-range naval gunnery, particularly by the British, made it necessary for fleets to fight at ranges far beyond the 5,000yd accepted in the nineteenth century. Range-finding required measuring distance, estimating the relative speed and direction of movement and the identification of the hostile vessel and its approximate size. That naval staffs had appreciated the need for reducing the conspicuousness of their warships by painting them a uniform obliterative colour was first noted at the opening of the Kiel Canal in 1895 when units of the French fleet wore a dark, and those of the German fleet, a warm grey. In 1903 the Royal Navy followed suit by changing its traditional colours of black and buff to a similar colour. In due course the Austro-Hungarian and Italian fleets adopted grey as a uniform colour.

But as Graham Kerr, with his naturalist's eye and special interest in warships, observed at Kiel the problem was 'not how to render the ship invisible in the strict sense—the normal background of sea and sky make that impracticable—but how to throw difficulties in the way of recognition (1) of the ship as a whole, and (2) of the individual details of its superstructure, for the latter are what are made use of in the group of operations which may be associated together under the term rangefinding'. His solution, which he tried unsuccessfully to get the Admiralty to adopt, was either to break up the continuity of the ship's surface or outline by violent contrasting pigments, or to use countershading by lightening shadows thrown by the superstructure.[6]

Making aircraft less visible while in flight gave rise to different problems not scientifically analysed until after World War I. In that struggle the aircraft was a new weapon of war and its capabilities and limitations had to be discovered stage by stage. M. Luckiesh, an American physicist, pointed out that the two general viewpoints of aircraft, from above and from below, demand contrary solutions.[7] While the earth's surface changes with season, and latitude, the sky may be clear blue, covered with dark or light cloud, hazy, or illuminated by the sun. Three factors therefore determine the colour of protective paint, and whether pattern should be used or not. These are the reflecting capacity of earth and water, the average colour of the land and the sea, and the brightness of the sky and clouds. Thus meadows, ploughed fields and woods absorb light and reduce reflection. Clouds lit by the sun may be brighter than an adjacent patch of blue sky, and according to their height, shape and density can act as a screen or a background. The higher up an observer ascends into the sky the deeper becomes the blue and brightness decreases. Over the sea, deep water reflects much less than shallow water, or estuaries containing suspended matter.

Not only does an aircraft's camouflage depend on brightness, colour, and size and shape of pattern, but on whether its role is to operate by day or by night. In daylight, surfaces should be dull and patterns more appropriate to sunlight than to dull weather. Upper surfaces should match the earth and lower surfaces the sky. An aircraft always appears dark against the sky. By night aircraft have to protect themselves against searchlights. While they are less visible against a moonlit sky when painted white, matt black is the best colour against probing beams. For aircraft operating over the sea, a dark colour is required and patterns are to be avoided.

In World War I the Germans were the first to take aircraft camouflage seriously (British experiments do not seem to have begun in earnest until early 1918). Following the principles just described (no doubt derived from Thayer), they painted the upper surface of machines operating by day a dull green, purple and ochre. Sometimes, after the theory of pointillism, they applied very small patches of pure colour, which were intended to mix with the background or blend into neutral tints. Under surfaces were either white, pale or turquoise blue, or pale blue-green. Occasionally, machines were decorated with polygons of blue, rose, yellow, green and mauve.[8]

The Germans were also the first to practise strategic bombing and their Zeppelin airships were often painted black underneath to reduce the visibility of the vast gas-filled hulls in searchlights. Likewise, the Gotha bombers which followed them were painted black, dark green, dull blue and wine. Sometimes a pattern of regular hexagons was designed, to which irregular patches of black were added.

The need to conceal movement from the air had already been appreciated, especially by the British Army in pre-war manoeuvres (on one occasion a division was 'lost' for some hours on account of the good use it made of cover). Against ground observers, fairly crude attempts were made to conceal the embrasures of coastal defences and the loopholes of pill-boxes.

1 DECEIVING THE EYE AND THE CAMERA

I very well remember at the beginning of the war being with Picasso on the boulevard Raspail when the first camouflaged truck passed. It was at night, we had heard of camouflage but we had not yet seen it and Picasso, amazed, looked at it and then cried out, yes it is we who made it, that is cubism.

Gertrude Stein.

To discover the object in time is no less valorous than to destroy it.

Red Star—Russian Army newspaper

By the end of 1914 the war on the Western Front had begun to assume the character which has become familiar to the generations succeeding the veterans of the British Expeditionary Force through the prose and verse of Graves, Blunden, Owen and Rosenberg; and the stark, haunted paintings of Paul Nash and Nevinson. A trench system, behind which lay all the paraphernalia of modern war, stretched from the North Sea to Switzerland, a form of siege warfare in which the two sides might be as near as 30 or as far as 800yd from each other. As Maj-Gen Fuller, exponent of the tank and military historian, has succinctly pointed out : 'It was the bullet, spade and wire which were the enemy on *every* front, and their geographical locations were purely incidental.'[1]

Not only did trenches have to be dug to shelter troops against bullets and shells, but emplacements for artillery, dumps for rations, fuel and ammunition, hangars for aircraft were constructed on a semi-permanent basis. Except where human traces were obliterated by shell holes, the movement of men and their vehicles and equipment over the countryside were indicated by their tracks and other distinctive marks.

Knowledge of what the enemy intends to do and the nature of his dispositions is essential and in World War I there were two instruments which greatly increased the range and efficiency of the human eye. One was binoculars and telescopic sights which could enable a rifle to hit a target accurately at a distance of 1,600yd. The second was the camera which, taken up in a tethered balloon or, better still, in an aeroplane to heights of 3,000ft and over could take photographs which, when interpreted correctly, provided information unavailable to the human eye. Not only could the camera cover a much wider area, especially from the vertical position, but it could record greater detail. On a black and white photograph the interpreter is not distracted by colour : earth shows up as white and grass appears black because it contains shadow and texture. Shadow and texture reveal the nature and location of equipment, buildings, and bare earth shows where excavations have been made and even the blast marks of artillery.[2]

Aerial photography had been practised since about 1909, principally by the French and Americans, though the Germans were probably the first to appreciate its military importance and specialised in using rapid and fine-grained plates. Used over the flat countryside of Flanders, with its chequer-board pattern of small fields, ditches and canals, it provoked the first developments of artificial camouflage. As early as September 1914 Guirand de Scevola, a fashionable Parisian portrait painter and certainly no Cubist, serving in the artillery, instead of covering the 75mm guns of his battery with foliage in the usual way, thought of using more permanent artificial materials. He acquired and painted canvas sheets, which were thrown over the guns when they were not in action.

The use of artificial materials for concealment impressed the French general staff and de Scevola was rapidly promoted from private to lieutenant and put in charge of the first camouflage section in the history of war. Fellow artists and designers were recruited to act as supervisors, factories were organised and civilian labour employed to prepare and paint canvas and other materials. At first de Scevola and his assistants disguised observation posts either by constructing dummy dead horses or cattle into which an observer could crawl and shelter while using his binoculars. Then trees stripped of their branches by bombardment were cut down at night and dummy trees substituted in which men could sit protected by steel plate and connected to base by telephone. The first dummy tree was set up near Lihors in May 1915 during the Artois battle.[3]

As aerial reconnaissance increased, so did demands from the front-line troops for camouflage. During the French offensive in Champagne, workshops were set up at Châlons and Nancy and new camouflage sections formed in all the armies, so much so that by 1918 about 1,200 men of all ranks and 8,000 women were employed by the camouflage service. De Scevola, who had by then been promoted to captain, and who made a point of always being elegantly turned out complete with white kid gloves, supervised the work and advised the general staff. Some of his ideas, it was said, took shape under the stimulating influence of a group of colleagues who foregathered at the Moulin de la Galette in Montmartre.

An English artist, Solomon J. Solomon, had, shortly after the outbreak of war, independently appreciated the possibilities of using artificial materials such as dyed butter muslin held up by bamboo poles to conceal trenches from aerial observation. He was then 54 years old, a Royal Academician and successful portrait painter. That fine painter and critic, Walter Sickert, held Solomon to be 'an academic in the good sense of the word', and although a traditionalist, he was broad-minded enough to encourage the young David Bomberg, who later became well known as one of the Vorticists.

Solomon, a member of a lively group in London society (his sister-in-law, Lily Delissa Joseph, was painter, pioneer cyclist, motorist and pilot), persuaded the military authorities to experiment with his nets at Woolwich and drawings of his proposals were sent to the commander-in-chief in France, Sir John French. But the general, then pre-occupied with what became known as the 'race to the sea', not surprisingly perhaps turned them down.

By the end of 1915 new ideas, such as the revolutionary tank, were circulating at GHQ. Haig had replaced French and already plans were being drawn up for what was to become known as the battle of the Somme. Solomon, who by that time had enlisted in the Artists' Rifles, was summoned to GHQ, France. British staff officers, impressed by what the French camouflage service was doing, wanted Solomon to be technical adviser to a similar British organisation. Solomon at once made contact with the French camoufleurs and found them to be congenial spirits after his own heart, as most of them like him had been students at the Ecole des Beaux Arts in Paris.

But Solomon's relations with the professional soldiers were less happy. He was soon to find out, like other civilians drawn into the military machine, that while senior officers were receptive, even enthusiastic, about his ideas, when it came to putting them into practice at lower levels, he met resistance of varying kinds. After an audience with Haig, who drew his attention to the importance of observation posts (OPs), he was taken to Plumer's headquarters at 2nd Army and instructed to make an observation post, similar to the French, on the Yser Canal. The banks were lined with poplars, willows and birches and Solomon made some drawings, at the same time undergoing his baptism of fire, eventually selecting a willow as a model.

He then returned to England to supervise the construction of the OP. The steel core, made of sections bolted together, was just large enough to hold an observer who mounted a ladder to his perch from where he could observe the enemy. Solomon designed it so that the part facing the enemy should appear too small for a man to ascend the tree (the French later copied this idea). The outside of the core was now covered with bark from a decayed willow in Windsor Great Park, after permission had been obtained from the King to cut down the tree. When ready for final assembly the trunk was screwed into a steel collar which would be embedded in the ground. The whole equipment weighed about 7cwt and required 12 men to lift it.

Solomon J. Solomon's impression of erecting the first British
observation post tree, 1916 (*Imperial War Museum*)

Solomon's next task was to form the nucleus of a camouflage
section. He sought out possible candidates in London not yet called
up for military service.[4] Among them was Walter Russell, an accomplished portrait painter and later a Keeper of the Royal Academy.
Fluent in French from his student days in Paris, he kept the French
girls in good humour as they tied hessian on to nets. L. D. Symington
used his gifts as a theatrical designer to design objects of deception.
Oliver Bernard, an artist–designer, was wounded and won a Military
Cross for his work in 1917. Earlier, though unable to swim, he had
been rescued from the *Lusitania* clutching a mascot. He died in April

1939, after joining a committee set up to co-ordinate air-raid precautions in industry.

Later arrivals included Harry Paget, a black and white artist, who went on to specialise in tank camouflage. More military than the others, he had been a star athlete in the Artists' Rifles. Ian Strang, who spent many hours in the front line making studies for OPs, was a painter and etcher of topographical subjects. Alan Beeton, a portrait painter, was one of the first to appreciate that the camera could be deceived by texture, but not by colour. Colin Gill, who liaised with the Canadian Corps, had also been a war artist and became well known for his decorations in St Stephen's Hall, Westminster. Leon Underwood, the sculptor, was more avant-garde than the others and offered his commanding officer designs after Marinetti and Wyndham Lewis. He was also a compulsive inventor and designed an automatic trench mortar. Among a number of theatrical property makers was Holmes, head property man at Drury Lane.

Solomon and his fellow artists were given temporary military rank, the former becoming Lt-Col. But a regular Royal Engineer officer, Lt-Col Francis Wyatt MC, then on the engineer-in-chief's staff in France, took charge of camouflage organisation. Wyatt had served in South Africa with a field company and had been in charge of mechanical units so that, although without artistic bent, he was well equipped to deal with the problems of camouflage in static warfare, which involved careful reconnaissance, large-scale manufacture of materials and their eventual transport forward. In this respect Wyatt was the father of camouflage in the British Army and both he and other members of his section were called on for their experience when another world war appeared imminent.

The camouflage section, disguised under the title Special Works Park, assembled at St Omer on 17 March 1916 with an advanced base at Poperinghe, but finally settled in a disused factory at Wimereux outside Boulogne. The factory had reputedly been owned by a German firm and, as a special railway line gave access to the works, had given rise to the rumour that it had been intended to provide cover, or camouflage, for long-range artillery to shell the coastline at Dover.

Wyatt's terms of reference were twofold: firstly to construct concealed OPs so as to be 'indistinguishable at close range from their surroundings and at the same time afford complete protection to the observer except from direct hit by high explosive; secondly, to cover trenches, guns, etc that required to be concealed from enemy observation by materials painted or treated in such a way as to make them merge into their natural surroundings.'[5] The second requirement is still today the basic purpose of camouflage.

Left: German observation post tree similar to the British and French OPs (*Imperial War Museum*); *Right:* plan for constructing an observation post tree (*Imperial War Museum*)

Until they became experienced, the British were helped by the French camoufleurs and before the latter returned to their parent unit won between them one DSO and five MCs, which indicated that camouflage work was not without its hazards. The camoufleur was required, for example, to crawl out into no-man's land at dawn or dusk and record the enemy's field of fire by sitting with his back to the German lines to sketch the landscape. These drawings were used to alter features and confuse the German gunners' aiming marks. And when the war artists, Wyndham Lewis and Augustus John, trying to find Ian Strang and imagining camouflage to be 'an admirable job', discovered that they were in the thick of the fighting they hastily withdrew in their staff car.

Meanwhile Solomon's willow was erected under his supervision and although the cross-cut saw broke its teeth on the old tree, the operation was completed without further incident well before dawn. Solomon later painted the scene in oils from memory.

The tree was, in fact, too small for an observer to use his maps or binoculars and later models were made larger. After reconnoitring a site for a 13ft-high OP disguised as a splintered oak in the notorious Ploegsteert area south of Ypres, Solomon turned his attention to tanks.

Col E. S. (later Maj-Gen Sir Ernest) Swinton was responsible for preparing the tanks (the name was chosen to disguise their purpose) in the summer of 1916 at Elveden in Suffolk, near Thetford, for their first operation in France. Swinton, himself an amateur artist, believed camouflage to be of the greatest importance.[6] The problem, according to Solomon, was to conceal or reduce the visibility of the tank on the way to its objective. Its rhomboidal shape did not help for 'under its belly was a square black shadow, impossible to efface except by some form of screen. Even though its upper parts might be made to disappear against some backgrounds, this black hole would be conspicuous, as all black shadows are, in a landscape for miles.'[7]

Solomon decided to paint a disruptive pattern of browns and greens to harmonise with the landscape (he went to the Somme Valley to make sketches). This might help to confuse the enemy gunners, but in dry weather the tanks would be obscured by clouds of dust. In fact, dust combined with smoke screens proved the most effective form of cover; the noise of the engines might be muffled by low-flying aircraft. Equipped with several tons of paint and helped by a detachment of 'painters', Solomon set to work, riding to and from the site on a pony, the only mounted officer in the 'least horsey unit in the Army'. Another form of camouflage was added while the tanks were in transit. On their sides, printed in Russian characters, were the words 'with care to Petrograd'. In France Russell and Strang supervised the painting of more of these cumbersome machines which were to operate in support of the Somme offensive; and in March 1917, the Heavy Branch, as it was then called, formed its own camouflage section under Paget.

Meanwhile, by 1917, the Special Works Park had become a recognised part of the organisation supplying the requirements of the four British armies then deployed on the Western Front.[8] Its main task was to provide artificial materials in the form of garnished nets and more specialised equipment such as fixed or portable OPs (the latter for trench parapets) and snipers' suits. Garnishing took place at two factories, at Aire near Hazebrouck for the northern sector and at Amiens for the southern sector. Subsidiary factories were located at Pont d'Ardres and near Rouen to produce reserve supplies. Garnishing, as already noted, was done by French girls recruited locally, many of them refugees from the battle area. While Russell provided them with designs they could follow, they were organised by British soldiers and at Aire by Miss G. Penrose of Queen Mary's Army Auxiliary Corps (forerunner of the Auxiliary Territorial Service) for which she was awarded the Military Medal. More specialised devices, which might be in the form of metal or plaster, were produced by the ingenious Symington at Wimereux.

Contact with the troops was maintained by the camouflage officers, who were either attached to corps, or visited units to discover requirements, give advice on siting and erection, and make reconnaissances for specialist work such as OPs. Otherwise it was left to the troops themselves to put up their own cover.

French girls garnishing camouflage nets for the Special Works Park
(*Imperial War Museum*)

In mid-1917 the Special Works Park boasted a strength of 60 officers and 400 other ranks. Demands from the front line increased as the troops began to appreciate what camouflage could do, the Canadians, in particular, being especially appreciative of new ideas on trench warfare. An outstanding example was the concealment of a dozen machine-gun posts at Monchy le Preux just south of Arras after the great German breakthrough towards Amiens in March 1918. It was vital to hold this bastion to prevent the gap becoming wider and the Germans hurled 11 divisions against the three Canadian divisions defending the sector. The failure of the German attack was attributed to two reasons: the Canadians had withdrawn the bulk of their forces from the salient so that the attack spent itself in vain and the machine guns holding the line were invisible from ground and air observation. They had been specially devised by Symington and had involved much deeper excavation than normal. The firing apertures existed only when the gunner was actually firing his gun and the gun was so far withdrawn from the aperture that the flash was almost entirely concealed. Five months later, when the Allies resumed the offensive, the Canadians were notable for demanding more netting than anyone else and made an important contribution to victory.

During big offensives such as the battles of the Somme and Messines Ridge it was almost impossible to keep pace with the demands for netting and the Park was considerably handicapped by lack of transport to convey materials forward or enable officers to reconnoitre. For the battle of the Somme 3,500sq yd of canvas had to be painted for 24 guns. The order was completed in fourteen hours, every officer and man taking a hand in the work. Sewing of the sheets, involving a mile of stitching, was done by one man on a treadle sewing machine. Later machinery was acquired both for cutting and painting canvas.

The painted canvas, which originated with the French, was far from satisfactory and when rolled up became highly inflammable because the linseed oil fermented. F. W. Jones, a chemist who had been working in France on poison-gas problems, was therefore attached to the Park to advise on the fireproofing of materials. It was discovered that calcium silicate deposited in the fibres of canvas by calcium chloride reacting on sodium silicate was a fireproofing agent. It was not long, however, before canvas was replaced, first by dyed raffia, which tended to shine and soon became unavailable because the stock from Madagascar ran out, and then by hessian dyed green and brown. This was cut up into strips 1ft long and 1in wide and garnished in nets purchased at first from fishermen at Boulogne. Wire-netting was used as an alternative and required less support and gave a more blurred outline than fibre nets. Hessian also had to be made fireproof after shelling at the battle of Messines had set fire to the screens, causing ammunition to explode.

Nets were, and remained, the most useful item of camouflage equipment, principally to cover artillery. At first, they were garnished equally all over, and held up by poles, ensuring that the flat top did not sag as it would make shadows (Solomon's idea). It was then discovered that the net cast a shadow and this was solved by garnishing thickly at the centre and thinning out towards the sides. Items of equipment such as ammunition boxes or cannisters were still visible

British howitzer covered by flat top net to conceal it from aerial photography
(*Imperial War Museum*)

from above and had to be covered individually with scrim. Nets also served to conceal ammunition dumps and to cover spoil from tunnelling operations. In the form of screens erected alongside roads leading to the front, they prevented the enemy from observing the traffic and, as gunners are disinclined to fire unless they can observe the fall of shot, they served a useful purpose.

In order to deceive the camera, scrim concealed tracks or simulated them, extending them to a dead end. Better than nets, was to site guns so that they could be reached over existing tracks or roads, or over ground already disturbed. Troops were trained to keep to these paths which would not then arouse the curiosity of the photographic interpreter. Blast from the gun muzzles left a mark on the ground and also had to be covered with brushwood or scrim.

Once the idea of siting batteries to conform with the landscape had taken root, nets could be used more imaginatively as sloping cover. Provided the guns were sited against hedges or banks, they could with the aid of nets merge into the background and it was possible to reinforce them with natural materials. Compared with the flat tops, they used less material, took up less space, and were easier to maintain.

In the winter of 1916–17 the possibility that snow would spoil camouflage had not been appreciated and snow fell through netting leaving an obvious black splodge, a fact immediately appreciated by enemy observers. In advance of the following winter, which was a hard one, stocks of white calico cut in strips were stored against the eventuality of snow. Blast marks were distinctive in snow and indicated otherwise well-concealed positions.

The specialised equipment prepared by Symington fell into three categories: countermeasure against snipers; disguise of snipers' suits; and provision of cover to enable a sniper or observer to see without being seen from a forward position. To locate the position of an enemy sniper, a dummy head and shoulders, realistically painted, was fixed to the end of a pole and raised above the trench parapet to draw fire. By putting a thin stick through the holes made by a bullet at front and back it was possible to make an alignment on to the sniper's position—provided he had not moved in the meanwhile. The more expert snipers, like the Scottish ghillies or Canadian trappers, tended to scorn these so-called 'mannikins', relying more on cunning developed through years of hunting to outwit their opponents.

In the second category, Symington painted transparent scrim garments for snipers which, combined with the wearer's skill in field craft, conferred invisibility from a few feet away. There were two varieties. The Symien consisted of a loose-fitting garment with hood attached, separate legs, a rifle cover and gloves. More convenient to the wearer was the boiler suit, which had a detachable painted hood and rifle cover and gloves. In September 1918, 44 of the former and 98 of the latter type were issued. Again, the experienced stalker might prefer to conceal himself with materials of his own choice but for the less-experienced these coverings undoubtedly helped.

Under the third category the equipment ranged from a concealed machine-gun post, in which the firing aperture appeared only when the gun was firing, to a combination of trench OP and sniper's post whereby, using thin gauze and sacking, it was possible to see through an aperture with no light showing to reveal the position. Other forms of headpiece or cowl used at short ranges were the Roland, Oliver and Beehive observation posts, each depending on careful camouflage for security.

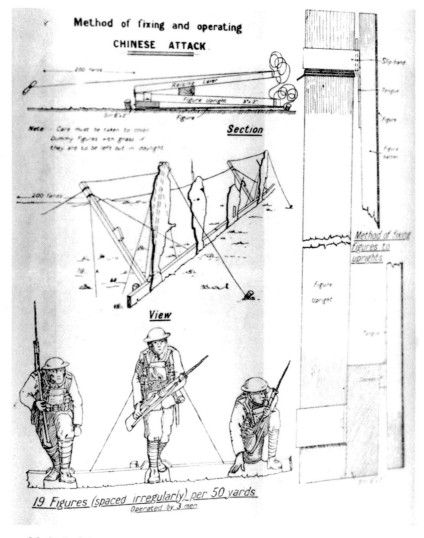

Method of fixing and operating a 'Chinese attack' on the Western Front
(*Imperial War Museum*)

Lifesize silhouette figures were occasionally used to provide a feint attack and divert attention from the real attack or raid. The figures, cut out of plywood, were fixed on the parapet and could be raised to an erect position in twos and threes as required, and then dropped again. When the figures represented men in various positions, they gave the illusion of an attack, especially when seen momentarily through the dust and smoke of battle. During the operations on the Messines ridge in June 1917, Special Works Park produced 300 dummy figures which were successfully used by 46th Division and in November they were used again as a distraction in the breakthrough at Cambrai. These so-called 'Chinese attacks' were revived in the Western Desert during the battle of El Alamein.

The Special Works Park was also required to assist in the erection of giant periscopes on the edge of large shell craters. The observers entered their post through a tunnel at the rear. Two 7ft-high periscopes were used by the Canadians in the battle for Vimy Ridge in April 1917 and another pair, 10ft 6in high, were put up on the forward slopes of Hill 70 during operations against the Hindenburg Line in September 1918.

By the spring of that year, plans were afoot to make camouflage less of a specialist branch. The increasing use of aerial photography pointed to camouflaging being accepted as a normal function of the soldier, who should not have to depend on the advice of the specialist camoufleur. For this, training of suitable officers was necessary and already a camouflage school in London was running courses. Equally important, it was necessary to dispel the mystery relating to the word associated with 'dead horses' or 'pantomime' and 'savouring of mystery and special technique'. Overwhelmed with demands for material, Special Works Park could not cope with such a task. Indeed, when Solomon visited Wimereux that summer, he was 'appalled by the monotony of production, practically all flat tops, of all one pattern, and put down without enough regard to nature of landscape. The photograph does not seem to be consulted. This place is nothing but a factory for production. No inspiration, no artistry, no grasp of the functions of camouflage.'[9] Symington told him that, in his opinion, 75 per cent of camouflage was utterly wasted because of lack of knowledge and because of standardisation.

At least a start was made in putting camouflage on a more scientific basis when orders were given to make a mosaic of air photographs covering the whole front, so that gun positions could be examined and new batteries sited with a proper regard to background. Unfortunately most of the proposals for organising camouflage on a corps and divisional basis were stillborn when Ludendorff launched his great offensive in March 1918 and threatened to break through to the Channel coast. Quantities of camouflage material and

Camouflaged mobile headquarters of Gen Sir Henry Rawlinson's Fourth British Army, 1918 (*Imperial War Museum*)

pamphlets on how to use it were lost in the retreat. When the Allies recovered their momentum the new title Camouflage Park RE superseded that of Special Works Park, though this did not signify any radical change in role.[10]

But more ambitious schemes were undertaken such as the camouflage of Rawlinson's 4th Army mobile headquarters (a train of twenty-four coaches) and the disruptive painting of aircraft hangars. One interesting task was the concealment of aerial ropeways then being tested in the 5th Army area. They were one of H. G. Wells's imaginative ideas, similar to the 'landships' or tank he had described in a pre-war novel *The War of the Worlds*, and long before the War Office had begun to take such a vehicle seriously. Instead of ration parties struggling through craters and mud to the front, supplies would be carried by an endless haulage rope supported by wooden poles and metal cross trees and driven by a small petrol engine. Where these ropeways ran alongside tracks, the problem was to make the latter less conspicuous. This scheme, which might have saved many lives, came too late to have any perceptible effect. Experiments were also made with dummy tanks called 'Tadpoles'. All that was required was a silhouette of the front of a tank which was held up at the back by a trailer fixed to it by bolts and braces. When the British reinforced the Italian front in the autumn of 1917, they were supported by a small camouflage section detached from Wimereux.

America had entered the war in March 1917 and shortly after two students about to graduate from Plattsburgh, inspired by the theories of Thayer, proposed the formation of a camouflage unit. They were Wilford Conrow and Homer Saint-Gaudens. The latter was son of a celebrated sculptor, Augustus Saint-Gaudens, and played a leading part in camouflage in both world wars. Pershing, the American commander-in-chief in France, after seeing what the British were doing, asked for a camouflage section to be sent to France. 'A unique and rather baroque institution' of sculptors, painters, advertising men and architects was formed by Saint-Gaudens and Conrow, leavened with technicians, carpenters, metal workers, scene shifters, electricians and a group of property men from the Hollywood film studios. Their training took place in the grounds of the American University outside Washington.

By September 1917 the American Camouflage Service, under Lt-Col Howard S. Bennions, had arrived in France and made contact with the British Special Works Park. Bennions set up a factory at Dijon, where large sheets of burlap were coloured and then cut into strips by French girls and tied into chicken wire. As many men as possible were given a fortnight's course in the art of concealment, both of themselves and their equipment, at a camouflage school at Langres under the supervision of Conrow. By that stage of the war the main purpose of camouflage was to deceive the aerial camera.

There appears to have been no organised German camouflage until after the battle of Cambrai in November 1917 but their application of it did not differ in any marked degree from that of the Allies, though they may well have made more use of structural camouflage. Attention to this aspect was drawn by Solomon, who displayed great interest in the discovery of what appeared to be an elaborately camouflaged airfield at the small Flanders village of St Pierre Capelle.

German engineers' dump concealed by straw matting during the retreat from Verdun, 1918 (*Imperial War Museum*)

When he examined air photographs through a stereoscope it appeared that an imitation field had been built up to the eaves of a house, as there was no cast shadow on the ground as with the other buildings. At the back of another house, its small garden seemed to have been raised to conceal a hangar.[11]

Solomon further suggested that the Germans had covered strategic roads to the front with overhead netting, in addition to screens along the sides, and that, during Ludendorff's March 1918 offensive, troops were hidden in large artificial shelters en route to the forward area to conceal them from reconnaissance aircraft. These claims for extensive area camouflage were investigated by the Royal Air Force, but aerial photographs failed to provide conclusive evidence, and Wyatt was sceptical. There was no doubt that the Germans practised the art of concealment thoroughly, though they sometimes neglected to cover the blast marks from their artillery, and in World War II, as will be seen, they made much use of supporting structures for permanent buildings. But in the field the labour required for such schemes would be enormous and a large force would be kept permanently employed maintaining them. It is more likely that the troops made good use of cover by day, restricting their movement to the hours of darkness. Solomon's enthusiasm for camouflage may in this case have run away with him, though after the war he expounded his theory in what may have been the first full-length study of the subject, *Strategic Camouflage*.

The possibility of a return to mobile warfare, with all that this implied in terms of imaginative generalship, seemed to be in the air in July 1918 after the failure of the final German attack on the Marne. As Wyatt tersely noted in his unit war diary the General Staff had at last recognised that 'the success of any future large scale offensive depends entirely on surprise'.[12] The use of surprise in the static warfare of the past three years had certainly been neglected, even if it had been possible. But there were two occasions when deception played a major part—the German crossing of the Aisne in May 1918 and, in another theatre of war, Allenby's masterly plan for defeating the Turks in the battle of Megiddo later that year.

After his great efforts to break through the Allied line around St Quentin in April and March, which so nearly met with success, Ludendorff set about choosing a new launching pad for another attempt to bring about victory. Although a renewed thrust towards the Channel coast would have brought a greater prize, the opposition was too thick upon the ground. Better to try a part of the front where a full-scale attack would not be suspected. Ludendorff selected as his point of breakthrough the 'blood-soaked ridge' along which ran the Chemin des Dames and which had witnessed so much bitter fighting since the beginning of the war. Now for many months it had been one of the quietest sectors of the Western Front. The French holding it had installed machine-gun nests which swept the bare slopes leading down to the river Ailette. So unlikely was it thought to become an active part of the front that five British divisions, recently engaged in the northern sector, were sent there to rest. As for the French troops, the local commander had so disposed them that they were heavily concentrated in the forward area, presenting a crowded target for the German guns, and leaving no reserve in the event of the front line not holding.

A German breakthrough, because of the virtual impregnability of this natural feature and its defences, would have to depend on 'secrecy and camouflage *in excelsis*' rather than on a lengthy preparatory phase, the usual procedure in operations of this kind. The assembly of the German divisions for the attack was planned with the utmost thoroughness and nothing left to chance. To begin with, the whole area was put under control of security officers, who ensured that the civilian population gave nothing away and stamped on any gossip among the troops. When the move into the forward positions began, wrote Liddell Hart,[13]

> Every artillery wheel had wood-wool wired on to its tyre; every axle was wired with a leather covering; every horse's hoofs were muffled in rags; every chain, ring, shield, or ladder was wrapped in straw. On the railways and roads, no vehicles were allowed to have a distinguishing mark, and troops made no movement by day except in small packets; and if these were on the open road when hostile aircraft appeared, they turned about, as if marching away from the front. The attacking divisions were brought up by nightly stages, hiding in woods by day.
>
> Nature provided a double reward for this care. For the difficult problem of bridging unnoticed the river Ailette which ran through no-man's-land was eased by the croaking of the frogs which swarmed in that valley. To this noise screen was added the greater help of a thick ground mist on the morning of the assault.

Some 4,000 guns were assembled, one of the greatest artillery concentrations of the war, to provide the opening barrage on a front of some forty miles.

The French suspected nothing. Only the American Intelligence Section, with a better deciphering capability, predicted the area of the attack, but because it was considered to be inexperienced, this information was discounted. And when the plan was disclosed by a German prisoner of war, under duress, it was too late to take the appropriate measures.

After a shattering bombardment the attack was launched at 1 am on 27 May and by the end of the day the Germans had advanced

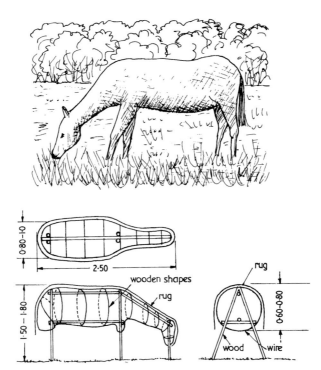

'Carcase' of dummy horse used by the Russians in Second World War as part of airfield camouflage, but not unlike the 'horses' used for Allenby's deception in the Jordan Valley (*Public Record Office*)

13 miles to the river Vesle. It was the deepest penetration made by either side since the beginning of trench warfare. By 30 May they were at the Marne.

Although from then onwards the German advance was stemmed by well-organised counter-attacks, the breakthrough showed what strategic camouflage really was, and how if it was to be effective, attention had to be paid to the minutest detail.

Allenby, a cavalryman, had no chance as commander of the 3rd Army in France to exercise any of the stratagems possible in a war of movement. In June 1917 he was appointed commander-in-chief of the Egyptian Expeditionary Force and his aggressive personality, though concealing a sensitive nature and the inclinations of a scholar, had in a short time galvanised his staff into making far-reaching plans for ridding Palestine of the Turks. A brilliant campaign, during which full use was made of deception, ended in the capture of Jerusalem that autumn, and when Allenby entered the city on foot on 11 December it caused a stir throughout the world.

The Turks, with German leadership and stiffened by some German troops, now had to be dislodged from the difficult country on either side of the Jordan Valley. Allenby's plan was no less than to sweep through to Damascus and beyond.[14] In the opening moves the British and Imperial forces made several thrusts towards the strategically important town of Amman on the Turkish left flank. Though they failed to dislodge the enemy, the latter became so worried about the possibility of another attack that he moved about one-third of his forces east of the Jordan.

From August to September 1918 Allenby concentrated his forces. His plan was exactly the opposite of the battle to win Jerusalem almost a year before. Then he had struck the Turkish left flank, while persuading them that he intended to break through on the coast. Now he intended to break through on the coast, giving the cavalry the opportunity to sweep northwards up the coastal plain. The Turks must be led to believe that the main attack would be delivered against their left flank. GHQ was moved to Jerusalem, camps were pitched in the Jordan Valley and additional bridges thrown across the Jordan. The cavalry was then ostentatiously moved into the camps, care being taken that they were observed by German reconnaissance aircraft and by ground observers. The infantry followed. Battalions of West Indian troops marched by day into the valley and were brought back by lorry to their starting line after dark. This operation was repeated about four times.

Next the cavalry rode out secretly and moved into their real positions in camps near the coast. The tentage had been increased some weeks before in anticipation, but after several weeks the Turks lost interest in developments in that sector. An illusion of the departed cavalry was provided by rear parties who erected lines of dummy horses made out of canvas stuffed with straw and suspended between ropes. Mules pulled wattle hurdles at the times when watering took place, raising clouds of dust. At night bonfires and lights shone in the deserted lines. Wireless traffic between GHQ and camps in the valley helped maintain the deception.

In contrast the greatest possible secrecy attended the concentration on the coastal plain. No movement was allowed in daylight. Irrigation channels in the orange groves provided water for most of the horses and the remainder were led to their watering points at dawn and dusk before or after the light was suitable for photography. The RAF patrolled the sky so effectively that hardly any hostile machines crossed the British lines. To mislead enemy agents, handbills advertising a horse show on 19 September, the day planned for the attack, were circulated in and around the camps. An intelligence map captured two days before that date showed that the Turks had been completely hoodwinked—there was no indication of the new assembly and on the contrary the Jordan Valley had been reinforced.

The cavalry were now given an opportunity such as had not yet occurred in the war. Quickly brushing aside slight Turkish resistance, one column rode over the historic plain of Esdraelon to the Jordan, another made for Nazareth where the enemy commander-in-chief escaped only just in time. Away on the right flank the Arabs under Lawrence harassed the Turks, cutting the railway at various points south of Damascus. On 31 October the Turks capitulated. In less than six weeks Allenby's troops had advanced 350 miles at a cost of a little over 5,000 casualties. But, as Wavell wrote in his life of Allenby 22 years later, 'the campaign had, in fact, been practically won before a shot was fired . . . the brilliant conception of the Commander, the handicraft of an experienced staff, had combined to prepare one of the most crushing strokes ever delivered in war.'

Reviewing what had been done, the General Staff, after the war, acknowledged that camouflage 'forms a branch of that important military organisation whose function it is to mislead the enemy . . . in accordance with the general plan of operations.'[15] We have seen that this was outstandingly achieved in the two cases described above. Though the actual application of camouflage had been crude and not wholly effective, it was realised that henceforward it must be practised 'as a matter of routine by all units'. But in the years following the art of camouflage was to be almost totally neglected.

2 DECOY AND DAZZLE

> The condition of the sea with its constant variation of light and
> colour is the ABC of the problem of concealment of ships.
>   Sir Edward Carson, First Lord of the Admiralty,
>   7 April 1917

The great sea battles between the British and German navies envisaged before World War I, in which the dreadnoughts with their
massive armaments were intended to play a decisive part, never took
place. Instead, it was a new weapon, the submarine, skilfully employed by the Germans (though breaking the rules of war), that very
nearly won them the war in 1917 and twenty-six years later nearly
won them World War II. The Royal Navy, unprepared for this
insidious type of attack on the lifeline to Britain across the ocean,
had desperately to improvise. In the face of opposition, the convoy
system was adopted in the early summer of 1917 and almost immediately reduced the losses of merchant ships. But there were two other
measures devised to defeat the U-boat which come under the heading
of camouflage: the decoy ship and dazzle-painting.

On 4 February 1915 the German naval staff imposed a 'war zone'
around Britain, similar to the British blockade in the North Sea, in
which hostile shipping would be attacked with all available weapons.
The U-boat campaign was slow to get under way, partly because the
Germans were able to muster only about thirty craft, and partly
because the German government was chary of operating too inten-
sively for fear of offending neutral powers, the United States of
America in particular.

Before the arrival of more scientific measures, one means of
combating the U-boat in this preliminary phase was the armed
merchantman. By the end of 1916 there were more than 1,400 such
vessels. They were encouraged to ram the enemy and rewards were
offered for the destruction of the latter. Better still, and it was
Admiral Sir Herbert Richmond, then Assistant Director of Operations
at the Admiralty and later celebrated as a naval historian, who seems
to have thought of the idea, deception might be used.

The hoisting of false colours has always been a favourite *ruse de
guerre* and decoy ships were not unknown in the Napoleonic Wars
as, for example, the Boulogne corsair in 1799 which drew alongside
a slow-moving merchant ship. Her reception was unexpectedly violent
when the 'merchant ship' unmasked her guns and fired a salvo at
point-blank range.

By the summer of 1915 the Admiralty had begun to fit out special service, or decoy, ships, which they thought might act as bait to entice the U-boat to close quarters where it could then be despatched.[1] A motley fleet was assembled at certain ports such as Plymouth and Scapa Flow and included a railway steamer, schooner, collier, tugs, and small tramp steamers. In 1916 small coasters, oilers and fishing smacks were added to the strength. Secrecy in fitting out and training the crews for their unusual role was all-important. The use of these Q-ships, as they became known (though one of the most successful captains, later a rear-admiral, Gordon Campbell, thought that this classification decreased rather than promoted the security of the operation), depended on a knowledge of what the U-boat commander would do on encountering his prey.

Three methods were open to him. He could, in the first place, attack by torpedo while submerged, but he would have to aim at his target through the periscope and this restricted him to looking in one direction at a time. In order to hit his target with a torpedo he had, at that time, to close to 2,000yd. Second, he could surface and use the gun mounted on the submarine's deck, but this took time for the gunners to go into action and also meant that the conning-tower was exposed. Third, he could surface and come alongside his victim, take off prisoners and documents and then blow up the ship. The policy at this stage of the war was to adopt the third method whenever possible: it was useful to bring back identification of the ship and torpedoes were expensive items of equipment and could miss the target.

Although the Q-ship was usually outgunned by the submarine when on the surface, at least there was a sporting chance of sinking it because not only was the conning-tower exposed, but the hull with its diesel engine batteries and tanks empty of water would be in full

Dazzle-painted British 'Q' ship—*Coreopsis* (*Imperial War Museum*)

surface trim. One hit on the pressure hull would send the boat to the bottom.

The Q-ship could either act as if she belonged to a neutral state, or she could fly the German colours, a much more dangerous undertaking. Nearly always, the first method was chosen. Her true colours were always flown immediately before she fired. On leaving port she would set course to frequented shipping lanes or to areas where U-boats were likely to be operating such as the south-western approaches, or the entrance to the English Channel from the North Sea. Care had to be taken that the Q-ship gave the impression of being on a voyage and was not merely aimlessly cruising. Ships were at sea for about a fortnight.

The armament of the Q-ship was carefully concealed. On some of the larger vessels a 12-pounder gun would be mounted in a dummy steering engine house. Three sides of the house were hinged halfway down so that they could be let down instantly. In one case the centre shutter was connected by wires to the flag mast so that the flag automatically came down when the order was given to fire. Up to four more 12-pounders were placed on either side of the ship. As it was then unusual for ships of that size to be equipped with wireless, the aerial had to be concealed as stays and halyards. Communication by wireless with base was to be used only in exceptional circumstances. At the same time every effort was made to intercept enemy signals.

Routine on board ship was carefully studied so that at all times it should appear to be an ordinary merchantman : only those needed to work the ship were allowed on deck in daylight; the gun crews were kept under cover and exercised at dawn and dusk, provided no U-boat was within sight or hearing. The log book and other confidential documents were kept in a special weighted box which would be thrown overboard if it appeared that the enemy was likely to board ship.

Ruses employed by the Q-ships varied according to their type. A fishing smack might be equipped with a well-screened 6-pounder and mingle with other vessels of a fishing fleet. On approach of the U-boat, a party of the crew would prepare to abandon ship. Meanwhile the gun crew were getting ready to fire, waiting for the order when the submarine was well within range and a successful hit appeared certain. Alternatively, a collier too small to waste a torpedo on, and therefore likely to be boarded and then blown up, would be equipped with two 6-pounder and two 3-pounder guns under command of a naval lieutenant. When the submarine had closed to within 800yd fire was opened. A third method was for a trawler to be disguised as a neutral cargo ship. She would be loaded with bags of sawdust, empty crates, timber and straw and derricks for loading and unloading at either end of the ship. She would be shadowed by a second armed trawler. In one such case the U-boat, after some hesitation, closed to within 1,000yd whereupon the Q-ship opened fire and sank the enemy with her crew. On other occasions the Q-ship was shadowed by a friendly submarine connected to the surface vessel by telephone cable, though the latter could foul the propellers of the submarine if care was not taken.

Very great risks were taken by the Q-ships to entice submarines to their destruction. Capt Campbell, one of the most successful Q-ship captains, actually sank three U-boats, but this involved the beaching of one Q-ship, another being towed into dry dock, and the third was sunk.[2] In the case of *U83*, his ship *Farnborough* was torpedoed without warning though her watertight bulkheads prevented her from sinking. The U-boat then moved towards the ship and inspected her through its periscope. Meanwhile the panic party had launched their lifeboat and rowed away. Twenty-five minutes after being torpedoed Campbell gave the order to fire. The white ensign was hoisted, the 3-pounders blasted away after their disguises had collapsed and a maxim gun stuttered from an hen coop on the aft deck. The U-boat was sunk. *Farnborough* was towed to port by a destroyer which had been hovering in the vicinity. After this action Campbell was awarded the Victoria Cross.

Later when commanding the *Pargust* his ship was again torpedoed, but thanks to her construction did not sink. After exchanges of fire with the submarine *UC29* she finally despatched her attacker. For this collective act the ship herself, which had suffered casualties, was awarded the Victoria Cross, an unusual distinction. There were many other acts of bravery performed by Q-ship crews in the highest traditions of the Royal Navy.

In January 1917 the German High Command gave orders for an unrestricted campaign on shipping. There was an immediate and almost catastrophic increase in the figures of Allied shipping sunk; the number of ships sunk by enemy surface craft also increased. The Admiralty's Anti-Submarine Warfare Division was already concentrating on better countermeasures, the most useful being acoustic methods of detection, paravanes, depth charges and mines. The number of Q-ships was increased to include 'every conceivable kind of merchant ship', including ketches, motor drifters, auxiliary schooners, sailing luggers and Brixham trawlers. An attempt was made to convert the Flower class of sloop to decoy ship, but they came into service too late to have any effect on the battle.

In any case by now the element of surprise had been lost. U-boats were less inclined to close with so-called 'neutral' ships because of the growing number of armed merchantmen and, with unrestricted warfare, torpedoed ships on sight. Moreover, as the armament of the U-boat improved, the Q-ship was at a hopeless disadvantage in fighting a duel and even the combined operation of Q-ship and submarine became increasingly risky. In August 1917 the Navy lost six decoy ships, including Campbell's *Dunraven* and the U-boat she had been enticing got away. No more U-boats were to be sunk by decoy ships, either on their own or operating with submarines, for the remainder of the war.

What contribution did the Q-ships make towards defeating the U-boat? The answer is very little.[3] Some 180 Q-ships operated and were believed to have accounted for 11 U-boats, only about 5 per cent of the total U-boat losses. Campbell, ever enthusiastic about the Q-ships' role, in which he had played such a distinguished part, claimed that they were put into operation prematurely, giving the enemy an opportunity to be alerted before sufficient numbers were available. The introduction of the convoy system more than compensated for the Q-ships' lack of success. Nevertheless, in a desperate situation every measure had to be employed.

A good deal of publicity was given to the story of the Q-ships in between the two world wars, inevitably damaging the element of surprise. Decoy ships were, it will be seen, used again in the opening stages of World War II, but this type of operation was soon abandoned.

Instead of giving hidden teeth to a non-combatant vessel, attempts were made to disguise destroyers as merchant ships.[4] They were called PQ-ships and sixteen vessels of this type were fitted out. Upper works were fitted to the destroyer's hull to give it the appearance of a small coaster. Two 12-pounders and one 4in gun were concealed about the ship. Later, all pretence of decoy was abandoned and the PQs were known as 'double-enders', both forward and aft parts looking alike. A dummy bridge aft and a single mast and funnel placed amidships produced this effect. Camouflage was added to confuse submarines trying to torpedo the ship.

Decoy ships were not used to any extent by the Germans, as Allied policy did not authorise attacks on merchant shipping, but they did adopt disguises for several of their surface raiders engaged in sinking merchant shipping. Naval cruisers operated in the early stages of the war, but one by one were picked off by superior Royal Naval forces. In 1916 the Germans resorted to the use of disguised merchant cruisers, which were used on a small scale throughout the war with considerable success. These ships posed as traders, flying the colours of neutral states and making use, on occasion, of wireless distress signals. They also altered their guise when necessary.

One of the most accomplished ships in this role was the 4,778-ton *Möwe*, able to travel at 14 knots and equipped with four 5·9 quick-firing guns, one 4·1in gun and 508 mines. In the course of two cruises she sank 42 merchant ships, amounting to 175,000 tons, and on her last cruise in 1916 escorted two Allied ships back to Germany. Hunting expeditions of other raiders produced fewer rewards. One of them was the full-rigged sailing ship, *See Adler*. In the end she was wrecked through negligence in the Pacific.

After the Admiralty had introduced the convoy system in April 1917, the enemy submarines were forced to penetrate the convoy escort in order to reach their prey and in doing so were vulnerable to gun fire or depth charge. Now that the merchant ships were under the control of the convoy commander, they could be made to perform tactics such as zig-zagging and, to add to thwarting the aim of the already harassed U-boat crew, they were painted with disruptive patterns. This was known as dazzle-painting.

Attempts to discover suitable means of reducing the visibility of warships at sea had been made by the Admiralty without much enthusiasm since the beginning of the war. Graham Kerr, mentioned earlier as being influenced by Thayer, believed the latter's theory of countershading could be applied to relieve dense shadows by electric light. Second, he thought that disruptive painting would break up the outline of a ship's structure if irregular patches of white were applied against a background of grey. This, he concluded, would reduce visibility and hinder the process of range-finding.[5] Although the Admiralty circulated Kerr's proposals to the Fleet in October 1914, leaving it to the discretion of ships' captains to put them into practice, it is doubtful whether any did so. Subsequent experiments with white and grey paint were not encouraging. A white paint believed to be suitable in Mediterranean sunlight merely increased reflection and made the vessel more visible than ever. Although Kerr continued trying to persuade the Admiralty to adopt his theory, he was politely but firmly informed in mid-1915 that because of the unpredictability of sea and sky backgrounds further trials were to be abandoned. Official policy was therefore to paint warships a uniform shade of grey whatever theatre of war they were in.

Another exponent of camouflage was P. Tudor Hart, a painter who had made an intensive study of colour values in Paris and had expounded his theories to a small coterie of artists in Hampstead before the war. Tudor Hart was generally critical of current military camouflage and explained that when objects on land were concealed they tended to absorb rather than to reflect light.[6] At sea the opposite occurred. He proposed to paint a geometrical pattern of alternating stripes of warm and cold colours, graded according to the area they covered. At a distance these colours were supposed to mix optically, assuming a general grey tone. Tudor Hart believed that because the colours were pure and arranged in a mathematical relationship they would 'fluctuate with the increase or decrease in light'.

As with Kerr, the Admiralty was inclined to be sceptical about the

'Dazzled Ships at Night'—painting by Norman Wilkinson
(*Imperial War Museum*)

outcome, pointing out that another series of trials conducted at distances of one to three miles by Mr G. A. Clark, 'one of the best known experts in the country' on orthochromatism in connection with photography of the clouds, had so far been inconclusive.[7] 'What most people do not realise', wrote the Secretary to the Admiralty to the Third Sea Lord on 4 April 1917, 'is that conditions at sea vary so much with the weather, that you can never be sure of having the same colour in the background two days running, and any colour scheme devised is liable to be upset on that account.'

However, their Lordships relented and Tudor Hart asked for, and obtained, four artist colleagues, then serving in the armed forces, to assist him. They were the brothers Sydney and Richard Carline— both serving in the Royal Flying Corps and both later to make paintings from the air which involved them in new aspects of perspective—Hugh de Poïx, and James Wood, a writer on aesthetics as well as a painter. But their experiments carried out with a pinnace at Portsmouth could not dispel the silhouette of the vessel and unless that was 'completely lost, the breaking up of the form by partial visibility is purposeless'. Like Graham Kerr, Tudor Hart also proposed the use of diffused lighting to countershade elements of a super-structure (an idea again seriously considered 25 years later). But for the time being Capt Clement Greatorex, Director of Naval Equip-ment, who was responsible for the trials, decided against further action. Similarly, other proposals of Tudor Hart's for concealing tanks and aircraft came to nothing.

At the same time as Tudor Hart and Clark were experimenting

with reducing visibility at sea, a young lieutenant in the RNVR, Norman Wilkinson, in peacetime making a mark as a marine painter and poster designer, had hit on what he claimed was an entirely new theory.[8] Wilkinson had served in the Dardanelles and was now serving on board a minesweeper in the English Channel, where he was able to observe the troopships sailing to French ports. They were all painted black—a colour which could not be more conspicuous to the captain of a U-boat, both by day or night. If ships could not be made invisible they could be painted so that their accepted forms were broken up by masses of strongly contrasted colour. This would be similar to the disruptive patterning used in nature and which Thayer called 'razzle-dazzle', an American slang term meaning to confuse. This dazzle-painting, as it became known, would make it very difficult for a submarine to decide on the exact course of the vessel it wanted to attack.

Norman Wilkinson's design for disguising an oiler—a favourite target for U-boats (*Public Record Office*)

Wilkinson wrote to the Admiralty explaining his theory, enclosing diagrams to illustrate it, on 27 April 1917. Evidently his letter found its way to the Admiralty Board of Invention and Research where it was pigeon-holed along with many other inventors' pet hobby horses. However, Greatorex, who had all along been doubtful about the possibility of reducing visibility at sea, rescued the letter. He was sufficiently impressed to allot a small store ship, *Industry*, to be painted white, black and blue according to Wilkinson's design. She was to sail in the Channel and orders were issued for any coastguard, ship, or submarine to report to the Admiralty on the weather and other conditions at the time the camouflaged ship was observed.

Although the essence of Wilkinson's theory was to depend on how a ship would be seen from a submarine's periscope, and this meant that the ship would be seen against the sky with little foreground, he had for the time being to be content with what was being done.

As the Admiralty had no facilities available where Wilkinson could develop his scheme for painting ships, if approved, he approached the Royal Academy. Within a few days he obtained permission to use four studios in the Royal Academy Schools at Burlington House. Meantime the U-boat campaign against Allied shipping was at its height. Eager to start work, and aware that the Admiralty would make no move until favourable reports on *Industry* were received, Wilkinson got in touch with a friend in the Shipping Division of the Ministry of War Transport. Without delay he was asked to appear before a committee chaired by Sir John Maclay, Controller General of Merchant Shipping. When he heard that Wilkinson had gone behind his back Greatorex was naturally furious. But the desired effect was obtained. Without more ado the Admiralty ordered that fifty troop transports should be dazzle-painted immediately. They would be used on the North American route, which was to become top priority for dazzle-painted ships. Furthermore, Wilkinson and his proposed Dazzle Section were transferred from the Admiralty to the Controller General of Merchant Shipping.

Wilkinson now collected a small staff of some twenty-five artists, designers and model makers, either over age or unfit for military service, and a team of girls to prepare colour charts. One room was set aside for viewing and a periscope was set up near a revolving table on which the model was placed so that the maximum distortion to upset the aim of the U-boat could be judged. The models, 1ft in length, were painted with washes so that changes could be made rapidly. When Wilkinson was satisfied with the design he instructed his staff to make a colour chart of the ship in profile on a scale of 1/16in. It was drawn on white paper, showing both port and starboard sides. The plan was then despatched to the port at which the ship was lying.

Design for merchant ship prepared by Wilkinson's Dazzle Section at
Burlington House (*Imperial War Museum*)

With experience Wilkinson evolved a number of principles on
which the plans were based. The light parts of the design were painted
with two light colours, each of a distinctive tone. The reason for this
was that there was a better chance of one colour harmonising with
the sky behind; it helped to distort the ship when used in conjunction
with black and dark greys. The most important parts of the ship to
distort were those near the stern and the fore bridge, both useful to
the submarine in determining the course of its proposed victim. The
bow end on the starboard side might be painted white and the after
end a shade of blue. These colours would be reversed on the port side.
It was important that a colour should not be allowed to stop at, and
therefore define, an important constructional detail, such as the stern,
or the centre of the stern. Thus either the white on the starboard side
or the blue on the port side had to be carried *round* the stern, until
checked by part of the dark pattern; the same had to be done for the
bow end. Sloping lines, curves, and stripes gave the best distortion.

As the work got under way, Wilkinson divided the Merchant Navy
into typical classes of vessel to facilitate painting. The section at
Burlington House made designs for each class of ship and the port
officers were kept supplied so that on the arrival of an uncamouflaged
ship, they were able to select an appropriate design.

The port officers (usually in the uniform of the RNVR) supervised
the painting of the ships. Those chosen for this duty were again
artists drawn from every quarter of the profession. At one end was
Edward Wadsworth, one of the Vorticists, and recently a naval
intelligence officer in the eastern Mediterranean, who jumped at the
chance of applying 'his experience of abstract patterning on a larger,
more functional scale than he could ever have dreamed of'. He was
later inspired to make some notable semi-abstract woodcuts on the
dazzle theme; and his work arising out of his experience as a camouflage designer has been assessed as being perhaps the 'last and most
spectacular manifestation of the Vorticist experiment'. Quite differ-

ent in outlook was Charles Payne, the black-and-white sporting artist known as 'Snaffles'. According to him, the execution of the design by gangs of workmen had to be strictly supervised, otherwise life-boats and carley floats were omitted. Some captains did not care for 'jazz' designs because they made their ships look slovenly and, Payne continued, 'ineffective and dangerous designs were all traced to the dazzle being painted by people who did not grasp the principle of the scheme'. In time, however, the foremen in charge of the gangs began to appreciate the finer points of camouflage.

Good reports were received from the first dazzle-painted ships taking troops across the Channel. Some captains, indeed, thought that the designs conferred some sort of 'magic' charm on their vessels. In October 1917 the Admiralty instructed that all merchant vessels and armed merchant ships should comply with the dazzle principle of painting. By the end of June 1918 the numbers of ships thus painted were as follows:

195 warships
2,112 British merchant ships
60 French merchant ships

Total 2,367

Wilkinson, in the meantime, had gone to the United States to impart British experience of dazzle-painting. Instructions had already been issued to American merchant vessels that they should be painted grey or dull stone. In October 1917 also, five systems were adopted: three had been proposed by George de Forest Brush, a painter colleague of Thayer (who himself had attempted to persuade the Admiralty to adopt countershading) and two other artists, Herzog and Mackay, and were based on reduction of visibility; and two devised by Toch and Warner, adhering to the principle of trying to confuse the aimer or observer. Failure to execute these designs resulted in an increase in the war-risk insurance premium.

In February 1918 a Camouflage Section was formed by the Navy Department within the Bureau of Construction and Repair. Like the British, the Americans were divided in opinion as to whether reduction of visibility or confusion regarding type, course and speed was more effective. But whereas reduced visibility required precise data about the kind of light, confusion of course for a given dazzle-painted vessel was something that could be estimated and checked in each individual case. The British system was therefore adopted. Top priority was given to troopships, destroyers, cargo and supply vessels and cruisers and gun boats in that order. Battleships were not camouflaged because they operated in formation and could be observed from a high vantage point such as a crow's nest from where it was impossible for an observer to mistake course and speed.

Some 1,256 American ships were camouflaged in the last eight months of the war.[9] In that period 96 ships of 2,500 tons and over were sunk. Of these only 18 were camouflaged. An analysis revealed that 11 were sunk by torpedo, 4 by collision and the remainder by mines. The Americans claimed that less than 1 per cent of dazzle-painted vessels were sunk by torpedo.

Meanwhile the Admiralty had set up a committee to find out how effective dazzle-painting was among British ships.[10] It reported in September 1918 to the effect that there were no material grounds to show that dazzle-painting had confused the enemy. At the same time statistics did not show 'that it was disadvantageous and in view of the undoubted increase in confidence and morale of Officers and Crews of the Merchant Marine resulting from this painting . . . it may be found advisable to continue the system though probably not under the present wholesale conditions.' The committee recommended that preference for dazzle-painting should be given, first, to ships sailing independently and, second, to ships, the owners or masters of which specifically required such painting. Finally, more attention should be paid to 'the study and perfection of individual designs for each vessel rather than to the number completed' (250 vessels a month).

This report provoked considerable discussion in the Admiralty which was now able to draw on evidence from the various theatres of war. In the bright Mediterranean light, for instance, dazzle-paint seemed to make ships more rather than less conspicuous, and at night the situation was even worse, non-white colours showing up particularly in contrast—and it was during the hours of darkness that U-boats were most inclined to attack. It was thought better to paint a ship a dirty white or grey with no contrast. Even more informed criticism was made by the Director of the Anti-Submarine Division. Experience had shown that the U-boat commander did not attempt to make a torpedo attack until he was within close range of his target and by that time camouflage could not disguise the main features of the ship and once the 'attacking submarine has passed abaft a bearing of about 5 to 6 points on the bow, the fore and aft features of the ship, ie masts, funnels, derricks, etc are of very little assistance in estimating the correct deflection for her torpedo and the athwart ship surfaces are her principal guide.' A good approximation of a ship's course, before diving, could be obtained from even one mast.

He did agree, however, that if the submarine commander had not appreciated the system and cycle of the ship's zig-zag before diving to attack, he would, provided the ship was dazzle-painted, and had only one mast and funnel, probably be confused until reaching a range at which the details of the ship were manifest whatever their colour. From another source came the information that dazzle-painting confused the enemy's aim sufficiently to make him miss the

SS *Montezuma*. Typical dazzle design for British merchant vessel, 1917–18
(*Imperial War Museum*)

vital spot (the engine room), whereas he had less difficulty with un-
treated ships. Post-war research seemed to support the sceptics and
in 1931, when German evidence had been sifted, the verdict was that
it was doubtful whether any submarine commander had misjudged
his target's course and speed through dazzle-painting alone.[11]

Masts certainly made aiming easier and the possibility of removing
or disguising them in some way was considered by Wilkinson in the
summer of 1917. Appreciating the importance of sinking oil-carrying
ships (usually three-masted), U-boat commanders had begun to single
them out for special attention. Wilkinson therefore proposed fitting
trysails on the aft mast, removing part of the mast amidships and
fitting a dummy funnel, dummy ventilators and canvas screens.
Only a few oilers, however, were fitted out in this manner, dazzle-
painting being easier to carry out.

Because of its morale-raising properties, the Admiralty decided to
retain dazzle-painting for the remainder of the war. The only exception applied to British vessels sailing to Scandinavia in convoy for
the dazzle-paint stood out among uncamouflaged neutral ships and
therefore invited attack. Nor did the order apply to vessels under
150ft in length. Assuming that a vessel would require two paintings
a year, the cost of camouflaging was estimated to be about £250–£300
a year. Dazzle-painting was largely restricted to the mercantile
marine though it was applied, without much effect, to the vessels of
the 10th Cruiser Squadron.

Wilkinson remained convinced of the value of his brain-child and
was awarded £2,000 by the Royal Commission of Awards to Inventors. As soon as the war was over, however, ships of the Royal Navy
reverted to their normal grey colour and in the intervening years
before the outbreak of World War II camouflage was quite forgotten
by naval authorities. A similar state of affairs existed in the US Navy.

3 THE THREAT OF THE BOMBER

Consider this and in our time
As the hawk sees it or the helmeted airman.
W. H. Auden, *Poems 1933*

According to the doctrine held both by politicians and military authorities in the early 1930s the bomber would always penetrate the defences of fighters and guns. By the spring of 1936 this assumption had already been undermined after radar had picked up aircraft 75 miles from the English east coast. This fact was known only to a tiny handful of senior officers and scientists and much more had to be done, not only to improve the early warning system but also to develop the organisation of reporting to the sectors and operations rooms which controlled the fighter squadrons awaiting take-off.

In the meantime the bomber presented a real threat, not only to the city centres against which a 'knock-out' blow was anticipated, but to the vulnerable factories and shadow factories then springing up, producing munitions and equipment, especially aircraft, and other installations essential for war. Camouflage was considered to be one way, albeit a passive one, of confusing the fast-flying raider as it dived through the clouds to locate its target, with the crew tense and probably tired after crossing the coast, thus compelling it to make another run and so exposing it to the anti-aircraft-gun or fighter defences. Little was known at this time of the difficulties involved in actually *hitting* well-defended precise targets, something rarely achieved with any degree of success even in the latter stages of World War II without radio or radar aids. Still less was known of the possibilities of locating targets with radio aids, making it unnecessary to identify them visually.

The art of camouflage tentatively developed in 1914–18 had been concerned in the main with movable objects rather than with static targets, and economies in post-war defence budgets had not provided for much, if any, experimental work. Even in Germany, while camouflage was taken very seriously by the army, the concealment of factories was virtually non-existent. Schemes for dispersal, however, were already contemplated.

Thus, in the autumn of 1936, there was little to protect factories and vital installations against sudden attack by the growing might of the German Air Force. A subcommittee of the Committee of Imperial Defence (CID) was set up under Sir Frank Smith, who had been first Director of Scientific Research at the Admiralty, and who was now Secretary of the Department of Scientific and Industrial Research (DSIR), to discover what the requirements of the services and civil departments were, but, more important, to organise camouflage on a national basis.[1] In addition to the service officers and officials serving on the committee, the advice of scientific specialists such as Graham Kerr, who was then playing an active part in politics as MP for the Scottish Universities, and Hugh Cott, the zoologist, shortly to be lecturing to senior officers, was called upon.

It did not take long for the committee to appreciate that to camouflage targets against reconnaissance aircraft would be a waste of time. The camera would not only 'see through' any attempt of concealment, but the location of most of the important factories, for example Rolls-Royce at Derby, the Bristol Aeroplane Co at Filton, or Vickers at Weybridge, were well known to the Germans. The possibility of infra-red photography, then in its infancy, was to be discounted for the time being (a number of experiments in infra-red camouflage had been made at the Royal Aircraft Establishment, Farnborough). Confusing the bomb-aimer was the main purpose of camouflage for static targets and, in due course, a rule of thumb was adopted. The target had to be made inconspicuous to an aircraft approaching at 180mph from a distance of 4 miles and flying at a height of 5,000ft, this being the average cloud base over Britain.

Oil tanks were particularly difficult to hide. Here two groups of oil tanks are buried each under a single mound (bottom right)

An aircraft flying above this height would be unable to see the target, while an aircraft flying beneath cloud level would be exposing itself to great danger.

The possibility of the enemy using radio aids, as happened when the Germans resorted to night-bombing after the Battle of Britain, or the possibility of hedge-hopping raids were not at this stage taken into account. In area-bombing, of course, camouflage could play no part. Until radio and radar aids became reliable, at a fairly late stage of the war, visual identification remained the best way of ensuring that the correct target was attacked. The feeling of the authorities before the war was that precise attacks were more likely to be made in daylight (although because of the limitations of the human eye in poor visibility, camouflage effective in daylight is equally, if not more, effective in moonlight). Despite rearmament being under way, the Chancellor of the Exchequer frowned on extending camouflage outside what was being done in the services—which was little enough.

The Munich Crisis in the autumn of 1938 blew a gust of realism through the speculative and somewhat academic discussions of the CID subcommittee. Overnight, air-raid precautions and civil defence assumed importance; runways and tarmacs of aerodromes in southern England were hastily given coats of green paint; vital factories were daubed with green and brown disruptive patterns regardless of the background and whether they were in any case identifiable from a neighbouring landmark such as a river, reservoir, or a tall chimney. Such amateurish efforts would be useless in war. The committee appreciated that schemes for concealing industrial targets would have to be tried out at once and experiments made to discover suitable paints and netting. Before it was disbanded early in 1939 the committee had recommended setting up an experimental camouflage section for this purpose.

Unfortunately, for some time before and after the outbreak of war co-ordination of camouflage was non-existent. In recent years the Chemistry Department of the RAE had developed techniques for making aircraft less visible in the air and on the ground and had extended its interest to evolving schemes for army equipment. It was therefore natural that the new experimental section should be set up at Farnborough. Wyatt, who had been in charge of camouflage on the Western Front and had recently retired from the Royal Engineer and Signals Board, was appointed director because, according to Dr R. E. (later Sir Reginald) Stradling, shortly to form a Research and Experiments Department dealing with technical matters of civil defence, he had a practical outlook and 'was not obsessed with the idea that camouflage can be indiscriminately applied to every building'.[2]

By this time, however, the Air Ministry had become seriously

concerned about the concealment of the aircraft factories so vital
to the expansion of the RAF. At the end of 1938 a section was formed
at Adastral House under Capt L. M. Glasson MC. Glasson had served
under Wyatt in France, where he had lost a leg, and after the war
had become a successful painter in the academic tradition. Convinced
that camouflage was important, he became a source of inspiration to
the small group of artists he gathered around him before the end
of the year.[3] They were Capt G. B. Solomon, nephew of S. J.
Solomon, the pioneer of camouflage, who had served as a pilot in
the Royal Flying Corps and became an official war artist, Cosmo
Clark, painter and later a member of the Royal Academy, Richard
Fairbairn, a student friend, and Richard Carline, who had been
involved with Tudor Hart's experiments and had also flown in the
RFC.

A large room was provided in Adastral House with a viewing room
adjoining, in which a balcony was constructed for viewing the models of
factories at the angle at which a bomber crew would see them. With the
aid of the Key Points Intelligence Department, set up in the Home
Office under Maj O. G. Villiers DSO, the Air Ministry provided a list of
factories and other installations of national importance and needing
protection in the event of war. Those of chief importance were known
as 'special cases' and subsequently defined as 'category 1A', those of
lesser importance as 'category B'. According to Carline, when their
location and plans had been obtained, it was agreed that for the
purpose of providing camouflage advice, firms would be asked to
provide scaled models in wood for the 'special cases' only; for the
'category B' cases, perspective drawings on paper would suffice if
aerial survey had established that camouflage would be effective,
and for all other cases, such as factories in fully built-up areas, a
simple written instruction with a chart of colours or tones including
red brick, grey and black would be issued. In order to decide on the
type of camouflage, flights were arranged through a private firm
at Hendon airfield, and aerial photographs supplied to supplement
observation. All this was highly secret.

Later in 1939, as war became increasingly inevitable, the
camouflage staff, which by then had an administrative headquarters
in Westminster, was increased with the recruitment of more artists,
including Geoffrey Watson, Tom (later Sir Thomas) Monnington,
subsequently President of the Royal Academy, Rodney Burn, also
an RA, Brian Thomas, a stained-glass designer, L. G. Stroudley,
Christopher Ironside, Richard Guyatt, Edwin La Dell and Stephen
Bone, all painters or designers. Leon Underwood, the sculptor, came
with his ideas on the need for structural camouflage, but temporarily
withdrew when he encountered opposition. A number of other artists
and art students were enrolled as junior officers or assistants. Artists

Well-camouflaged factory showing disruptive painting and screens to hide shadows cast by building and to conceal stores placed outside
(*Public Record Office*)

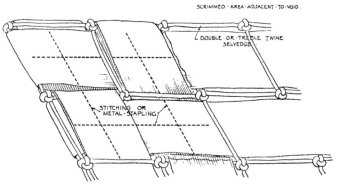

SCRIMMED · AREA · ADJACENT · TO · VOID.

DOUBLE · OR · TREBLE · TWINE SELVEDGE

STITCHING · OR METAL · STAPLING

· ENLARGED · DETAIL · OF · CORNER · OR · END · FIXING ·

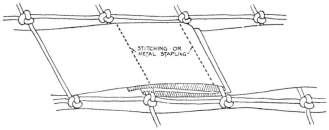

STITCHING · OR METAL · STAPLING

· ENLARGED · DETAIL · OF · JOINTING · SCRIM ·
(SHORT · ENDS · OR · CHANGE · OF · COLOUR)

·STANDARD·CAMOUFLAGE·NETTING· ·METHOD·OF·SCRIMMING·NETS·

C.D.C.E. LEAMINGTON SPA   DRAWING Nº 98240

Method of scrimming standard camouflage net (*Public Record Office*) made good camouflage designers because they were able to analyse and memorise what the target looked like from the air.[4] Being trained to create depth and distance on a flat canvas or paper, they were better able to reverse this process by disrupting the characteristic form of an object. They had to remember that the target might be seen at 2,000 or 20,000ft so that their design had to compromise between the two viewpoints, ensuring that shapes and tones looked convincing at high and low level.

After discussions with the National Paint Federation, mainly through Dr L. A. Jordan, a type of paint which would not shine was manufactured in a prescribed range of 14 colours or tones—brown, green, grey, black and red brick. During the eight months preceding the declaration of war, about 700 factories were listed, of which more than 100 were treated as 'special schemes' with scaled models constructed. It was not until July 1939 that special powers were obtained to compel factory owners to carry out their camouflage instructions, for which 50 per cent reimbursement was allowed.

In September 1939 the Air Ministry's camouflage section was taken over by the Home Office, and shortly afterwards by the Ministry of Home Security, which became responsible for all aspects of civil defence. The following month it moved to Leamington Spa and assumed the name of the Civil Defence Camouflage Establishment.[5] Many of the staff continued to paint in their spare time and at weekends. The camouflage designs were prepared in a large hall known as the Rink and a special viewing balcony was erected like the one at Adastral House. For daylight viewing, models were constructed so that they appeared as if seen from 20,000ft away, or nearly 4 miles. Foreground and background appeared on a painted cyclorama and direct and diffused lighting was provided. Later, a German bomb-sight set up on the viewing platform gave an idea of how a target appeared to an enemy aircrew.

When night-bombing began in earnest, the distinguishing of features at night had to be learnt.[6] Lamps provided with colour-correcting filters provided varying kinds of illumination and a special box called a 'moon-cluster' enabled an observer to examine models down moon, up moon and across moon. Targets in misty conditions were examined through a haze box. The models made under the supervision of Ironside had to be presented on a turntable so that they reflected the light in the same way as the full-scale camouflaged factory, and paint and texturing had to be simulated exactly.

A viewing tank for conducting experiments on sea-going camouflage was set up at the request of the Admiralty with the capability of simulating atmospheric conditions at home and overseas. A naval camouflage section under Cdr J. Yunge-Bateman RN, also an artist, and one of Glasson's original staff, together with Mr Trice Martin, a veteran of World War I, and Wilfred Shingleton, a film producer, carried out the tests, but much of the optical equipment was devised by a brilliant young scientist, A. E. Schuil.

The administrative staff was housed in the Regent Hotel, requisitioned for the purpose. Glasson always came to the Rink to inspect the models, revealing a considerable critical faculty. Aerial surveys, through the RAF, which provided a few small and not always reliable aircraft, were made from Baginton airfield nearby.

Carline recalls that the camouflage officers were frustrated by the long delays between their completion of the camouflage scheme and its actual execution on site. The accepted procedure was to instruct a firm to obtain tenders for the work from three separate contractors. These were then submitted to the Regent Hotel. In some cases they might be presented in the wrong form; delays of several months before approval was given were usual. It was not until a year later that the process was speeded up. This slowness in implementing camouflage was one of the reasons for the new Ministry of Aircraft Production taking over measures for the factories for which it was responsible.

Visits to important installations to supervise and speed up camouflage measures were not generally approved. The design, specification and approval of tenders was done by different sections. Eventually this slow procedure was accelerated by the camouflage officer visiting the factory at the invitation of the firm for whom the scheme had been prepared. These included Rolls-Royce at Derby, Handley-Page, Vauxhall Motors at Luton and others. It was when painting the model for the Rolls-Royce parent factory at Derby in May 1939 that Carline had to simulate its urban surroundings of small houses and their gardens, and he sought to disguise a very conspicuous high building as a church, providing it with a false steeple. He felt somewhat ashamed when Glasson, very rightly, disapproved, pointing out that it would justify enemy attacks on churches. Meanwhile Geoffrey Watson spent time at the Bristol factory at Filton and Monnington worked at Vickers-Armstrong, Brooklands, including the highly conspicuous motor-racing track.

When new factories were being built after the outbreak of war, aerial surveys showed that their exposed sites with large areas of excavated ground, the top soil buried, rendered them extremely vulnerable. This was the subject of much concern and debate and it was eventually urged that camouflage advice should be sought as soon as construction was planned and even in the choice of site. Of some 123 new factories built in 1940 and 1941, in only a very few cases had concealment been considered at the outset. Notification was received too late, as for instance at the Parnall aircraft factory at Yate when camouflage advice was ignored during construction. It was totally destroyed by bombing before it could be used.

Example of structural camouflage designed by the Civil Defence Camouflage
Establishment, Leamington. The nets screen shadows cast by the building
(*Public Record Office*)

With the growing recognition that paint alone did not provide
adequate concealment, the need for structural measures such as
screens of scrimmed netting, use of granite chippings, and other
textural materials such as steel wool (fastened on to galvanised
wire-netting) were considered and qualified architects and engineers
were added to the staff at Leamington.[7] A special Camouflage and
Decoy Section was set up at a separate headquarters under Prof
W. E. Curtis, who had fought at Gallipoli and had been teaching
physics at Durham University. Two other physicists, Dr R. A. Sayce
and Dr T. A. Littlefield, assisted him. Rodney Burn was transferred to
the new section for advice and aerial survey; he was joined by Brian
Thomas, Monnington and William Morgan. Leslie Watson was also
transferred as adviser on horticultural experiments.

Several months before the outbreak of war William Hayter, painter
and engraver, with John Buckland-Wright, Roland Penrose and
Julian Trevelyan, all painters, and Denis Clarke-Hall, an architect
who later joined the Leamington staff, formed an Industrial
Camouflage and Research Unit.[8] They set up as independent
camouflage consultants in Bedford Square, London—unaware that
camouflage had been authorised by the government for all vital
factories—and they were not permitted facilities for flying without
which no camouflage design could be adequate. Trevelyan later
readily admitted that a lot of their assumptions were 'false and that
the pattern of the world from above is read very differently from the
way in which we had supposed'. However, because of Hayter's
persistence, they found a client who wanted a big factory in the
Midlands concealed.

They climbed all over the buildings, then made a model, and back
in their office produced a scheme which was in effect 'a huge abstract
picture painted over the roofs and chimneys of an industrial town'.

But, as the much-heralded air raids did not occur in the first winter of the war, their clients became less enthusiastic and, though they paid for the designs, they were never carried out. Unofficial camouflage as practised by Hayter's group was officially forbidden in 1941 after fire had broken out at a firm not on the vital list through the use of combustible materials in an unauthorised scheme.

During this period of the so-called 'phoney war' there was a good deal of criticism of official camouflage by scientists such as Graham Kerr[9] and Cott (the latter had been asked to camouflage an East Anglian airfield but the experiment had proved far too elaborate and expensive). This campaign was conducted in Parliament and in the pages of *Nature*. Much of the criticism was based on the argument that camouflage was not observing the principles of nature in the first place and, secondly, that more scientists and engineers rather than artists should be employed. It took a scientist, T. R. (later Sir Thomas) Merton who, in addition to being involved in war research, was also a connoisseur of painting, to point out that camouflage was a matter of common sense, each target differing from the other just as one face differed from another.[10] For that reason the artist, whether standing back from his easel or looking down from an aeroplane, drew on his experience and from trial and error when making his design. Engineers, chemists and physicists were all needed to solve the practical problems.

Since before the outbreak of war a plethora of government committees had tried to resolve the problem of co-ordinating civil and military camouflage without success.[11] At last, in May 1941—by which time daylight had given way largely to night raids—a committee on concealment and deception under William Mabane, Parliamentary Secretary to the Minister of Home Security, drew attention to the need, already noted, to reduce the time before a vital target was effectively concealed. Arising out of its recommendations a new camouflage committee was set up to promote unification of design, practice and methods of maintenance and the fullest technical co-operation in all departments.[12] Chairman was Wing-Cdr T. R. Cave-Brown-Cave, who had just been appointed executive and administrative director at Leamington. He was professor of mechanical engineering at Southampton University, and closely associated with airship development before the war. It was thought that his reputation would carry weight when working with other departments.

The secretary of the camouflage committee was the painter Robin Darwin, a member of the illustrious Darwin family and who, when not on duty, would set off in an open Rolls-Royce, wearing a wide-brimmed black hat, to sketch the countryside. This mildly Bohemian behaviour caused him on one occasion to be arrested as a spy in company with Leon Underwood.

On account of the importance of materials and their supply, a technical subcommittee had been formed in May 1940 under Curtis and, among other matters, dealt with smoke, the concealment of water, and alternatives for screening material such as hessian and steel wool.[13] One of these was alginate fibre derived from seaweed and it was believed that the alginic acid might be proof against infra-red photography. It was also non-flammable and for these reasons was called BG (Bloody Good). BG could either be spread between wire-netting like a sandwich, pegged down on the ground, or used in strips to garnish nets. Unfortunately it was subject to bacterial decay; cows (it was said) liked to eat it; it shrank on wetting or drying; it was very brittle; and it deteriorated fairly rapidly through weathering. Steel wool, of which there was a surplus at this stage of the war, was preferred by the Army and, as aerial infra-red photography did not then appear to be a threat, in June 1944 development of BG for warlike purposes was abandoned.[14]

In fact, far less sophisticated materials, like sludge, in the end proved cheaper and just as effective. The residue of oil from ships' tanks could be used to darken all kinds of surfaces from roofs to runways and inspired one of the technical members to doggerel verse:

Sludge! Sludge! Glorious Sludge
Scraped from the bottom of tanks;
Lots you can do with it, have a shampoo with it,
Rub the old back with it, paint the town black with it,
Charm away bunions, fertilise onions,
Massage the cranium, good for the brainium!

And so on.

The switch of the Luftwaffe to support the attack on Russia enabled camouflage to be relaxed gradually. From the end of 1941 only the most vital targets, and of those only 440 out of 800, considered essential to the defence of the country, were treated with high-grade camouflage; all other buildings were to be concealed against night-bombing only and this meant a general toning down of shiny surfaces. Camouflage was now intended for the occasions when the enemy's navigational aids had broken down and for targets in the coastal belt where daylight raids were still carried out on a small scale.[15] Radar cover and British air superiority had made it improbable that the Germans would be able to bomb undisturbed.

The unlikelihood of massive enemy air raids had, by March 1943, decided the government to order camouflage to be reduced by 50 per cent and this was made doubly necessary by the need to conserve manpower and materials. The Baedeker raids of the summer of 1943 were a further indication that the Germans were no longer capable of pin-point bombing. Henceforward, if camouflage was to be used at all, it would be as protection against brief attack against particular targets and these were mainly to be found on the south coast, where preparations for returning to the Continent were now in motion. Interest now centred on the need to deceive the enemy as to where the landings would take place. In the offensive by pilotless aircraft and rockets against southern England in the last stage of the war, camouflage had no part to play as accuracy was not a criterion for success.

Some members of the Camouflage Directorate were now involved in an offensive rather than a passive role.[16] The radio and radar navigational and bombing aids which would in the end make it unnecessary for the crews of Bomber Command to identify their target took time to develop. Until 1943, if not later, targets in Germany still had to be identified visually. Crews had to be trained to see by night. Leamington was called upon to make realistic models, showing such features as target indicators, incendiaries, bomb flames, searchlights, flares and decoys. Brian Thomas, who had written a pamphlet for civil defence, *Aerial Observation at Night*, now adapted it for bomber crews.

When in 1943 target-indicator marking was introduced in Bomber Command, individual aircraft of the main force no longer attempted to identify targets visually, but aimed their bombs at markers dropped by the pathfinders. The question then arose whether crews were identifying the indicators correctly. Tom Monnington flew on target-indicator demonstrations, and subsequently on operational sorties, in order to make paintings of the indicators and schematic drawings showing markers at various stages of burning. Slides were made from these paintings and drawings showing different types of attack and indicating the conditions in the area such as the glow from fires, haze, and background. They were later replaced by more effective methods which included the use of transparencies, but at the time they served a useful purpose and were used at operational training units and for briefing at operational bases.

Throughout these years American factories had been producing war equipment of all kinds, and for Britain even before America was officially at war with Germany. Some reference has been made to American military camouflage, which in the inter-war years had fallen into desuetude as in other armies. The urgent need to conceal some of these vital sources of production suddenly became apparent after the traumatic experience at Pearl Harbor on 7 December 1941. Thereafter a surprise attack from Japanese carrier-borne aircraft operating off the west coast against the aircraft factories of Douglas at Santa Monica, Los Angeles, or the Boeing plant at Seattle could not be discounted, while on the east coast the possibility of a German raid against the Martin plant at Baltimore had to be taken seriously. A small group of artists and architects, working in close collaboration with the military and civil defence authorities, were employed full-time to disguise these targets sufficiently to confuse the enemy and make pin-point bombing difficult, if not impossible. Likewise, the Canadians decided to conceal a major aluminium plant on their east coast and Ironside was flown across the Atlantic to advise.

Some fifteen to twenty American airfields within 300 miles of the east and west coasts were also camouflaged. And on the east coast there was the possibility of German U-boats and naval surface craft bombarding inshore targets. Coastal batteries and installations in bases down the West Indian chain of islands to British Guiana, which the Americans had taken over in exchange for fifty destroyers required by the Royal Navy, demanded concealment and so did the batteries defending the Panama Canal. All these targets required static camouflage and their treatment did not differ in any great degree from that to be described in the next chapter.

4 DEFLECTING THE BOMBER

Camouflage is an essential weapon of defence.
The Camouflage Committee, 5 March 1942

As the national economy became geared to the production of war materials the number of vital factories increased and by mid-1943 there were no less than 8,000 of all categories on the list. However, over a year before, in January 1942, the Civil Defence Committee, which had now taken over the supervision of camouflage from the Mabane Committee, appreciated that a much more stringent classification was required on account of the quantity of men and materials needed. It therefore agreed to set up the Civil Camouflage Assessment Committee, on which the various ministries were represented, to define scales of camouflage for buildings and installations according to their importance and location.[1]

The most usual category was for 'night' which required no more than a general reduction of conspicuousness by dark paint, usually black. Factories in the 'night plus' category had to be given more sophisticated treatment with patterned paint and textured roofs and occasionally structural camouflage. Vital factories were given a category of 'day' or even 'day plus', which meant they were to be given structural camouflage and painted with a disruptive pattern. Targets in the latter two categories were few in number and usually situated in south and south-east England within easy range of the enemy.

Treatment of factory buildings depended on their situation.[2] In semi-rural surroundings a disruptive pattern echoing the nearby green or brown fields and dark woods was carried over the roof and sides of the buildings. Shine on roofs, glass and the light colour of roads leading to, and yards or open spaces surrounding, the factory had to be made less conspicuous by staining with paint or other forms of darkening substance. In towns or built-up areas, surrounding features such as a housing estate, rows of small houses or roadways were imitated.

Roofs were first treated with paint mixed with grit in order to reduce shine, but this was found to provide insufficient texture and was replaced by black shale, or preferably granite chippings to give greater depth. These aggregates were fixed to the roof by adhesives of coal tar or bitumen in the form of an emulsion or solvent.[3] More expensive forms of roof-covering were: woven wire, garnished with steel wool and held in position by steel wires (the steel wool had to

Pitched roofs were extremely conspicuous from the air and had to be hidden by netting combined with disruptive paint work (*Public Record Office*)

be spray-painted black and periodically treated for rust); coir-netting, a form of coarse vegetable fibre spun into a yarn and woven into a mesh by means of an adhesive of coal tar or bitumen; or there was a plastic paint called Arpex, given a rough texture before it set by brushing it with a stiff broom.

It was essential to eliminate shadows cast either by walls or pitched roofs, which were often erected in rows forming a saw-tooth pattern. Structural camouflage was the best way to treat such cases. Netting was suspended horizontally from a roof ridge or from the eaves of a building. Nearby car parks, water tanks and other installations had to be similarly covered. Netting was arranged so that it caught the light and matched adjacent surfaces of the building and the sur-rounding ground in both tone and colour. Covering was either furnished by string-netting, garnished with strips of dyed hessian, woven wire-netting garnished with pre-coloured chicken feathers glued to it, woven wire garnished with steel wool, or pre-coloured coir-netting. The last-named was the most suitable for it combined rigidity, flexibility and good weathering properties. Where roofs were covered with highly inflammable materials such as bitumen or felt a special fireproof scrim was used. Factory chimneys were usually painted a light colour near the top and their long, vertical shape was broken by irregular dark bands; the north side was painted light in tone to counteract the shadow.

Special attention had to be given to the concealment of petroleum

Camouflaged concrete runway showing paint work and touch-down marks of aircraft (*Public Record Office*)

tanks.[4] They were unmistakable objects, reflecting the light from their tops and their circular sides casting shadows. The use of netting to eliminate shadows presented a fire danger, though steel wool, which was non-inflammable, was a good alternative. Tank farms, more often than not, were situated close to conspicuous areas of water, rivers, or estuaries such as the Thames. A variety of schemes were tried, including the use of compressed asbestos to give an irregular shape, and the painting of cast shadows. Generally, light tones rather than dark were preferred for the structure itself. In the end the Petroleum Department decided that the only effective means of concealment was to bury tanks, wholly or partially, below ground level. This, of course, could be done only to new installations. By October 1941 the main bombing threat had fortunately passed and, apart from painting and texturing existing tanks, no further action was taken.

The responsibility for camouflaging airfields, civil and RAF, was divided between three agencies. Certain airfields attached to aircraft factories such as Castle Bromwich, Heathrow, Radlett and Brooklands were, as has been seen, taken on by the design section at Leamington and by Monnington and Rodney Burn in particular. But most of them came under the responsibility of the Ministry of Aircraft Production (MAP) in the summer of 1940, when the completion of new fighter aircraft was vital for the country's survival. A factory defence section was organised by Cdr Stephen King-Hall, the well-known broadcaster and independent MP. Carline, because of his experience of flying and painting from the air, became its technical adviser and also acted as a liaison officer between MAP and Leamington, attending the various committee meetings held there.[5]

In 1941, when the MAP became responsible for camouflaging 'shadow' factories and the airfields attached to them, Carline organised a small department for this purpose, his staff consisting of architects and horticulturists. They superintended the application of such measures as texturing of runways and aprons, selective seeding of grass and clover, construction of artificial hedges on parts of an airfield, differential mowing to provide alternate areas of long dark grass and closely mown light grass with brown painting to give the effect of plough, together with dummy roads and paths. Such schemes at airfields, numbering about twenty-seven, required special equipment and regular maintenance by his staff. Satellite landing grounds for the storage of aircraft also had to be concealed and various types of hide (or 'robin' hangars) were devised, which could take nets to aid in concealment.

Thirdly, the responsibility for concealing operational airfields rested on Col J. F. Turner, a retired Royal Engineer officer, who since 1931 had been Director of Works and Buildings at the Air Ministry. Turner, or 'Conky Bill' as he was more familiarly known, had been a resourceful member of the original CID camouflage committee. He endeared himself to the airmen because he had learned to fly; he was ingenious and ruthlessly cut through red tape. A one-time RAF station commander recalls his arrival at Manston with a gang of men, either past military age or unfit for active service, who with the aid of a contraption like a spinning jenny rapidly covered the huts and other buildings with various tones of paint including, unhappily, a number of airmen's uniforms which had been hung outside after cleaning in preparation for inspection. As will be seen, he also became responsible for decoys and from the end of 1942 ran his own department in the Air Ministry dealing with camouflage and decoy. By then his services had been rewarded with a knighthood. Turner employed a flight of aircraft at Hendon for making surveys.

Before the war RAF stations had been built without any regard for concealment. Constructed of light Fletton brick, they were invariably conspicuous, standing usually at the edge of a large green expanse of some 250–300 acres (concrete runways did not then exist). Surrounded by the natural multicoloured fields of the English countryside, nothing could give a clearer indication of an airfield.[6] Various measures were devised, the more effective ones requiring much materials and labour. In the Munich Crisis large quantities of 'anyone's water paint were applied to represent hedgerows and fields'. After the outbreak of war experiments were made with bituminous paints and surface dressings which included a mixture of sawdust, soot and oil. This proved to be more lasting than hedge-painting. Sand was spread on runways but after a time caught the light. Even straw was used to alter the tone and colour of grass runways, but was soon dispersed by the slipstream of aircraft. Sulphate of ammonia darkened the colour of grass and was effective during the growing period in the spring.

Turner, unlike some others, believed that structural camouflage could be useful.[7] He made dummy hedgerows, including a T-shaped upright 3ft high with 2ft-long cross-pieces. Brushwood was placed in the supports, the dummy hedge being secured by wires. The pattern of the hedge followed the character of the existing hedges in the area. On other occasions dummy woods were erected, using felled trees up to heights of 30ft realistically painted with spray guns.

In due course heavier aircraft came into operation, requiring concrete runways, and this taxed the ingenuity of the airfield committee at Leamington. Darkening by paint or stain was not altogether effective and recourse was had to surface dressings. Sawdust stuck down with bitumen lasted for only a short time. As for harder materials, something was required which did not cause excessive wear to aircraft tyres. Wood-chippings obtained from scrap timber, rubber particles and granulated rubber were all used to give texture and reduce shine. Another original solution was to bore holes in the concrete runway in the course of construction; they were then filled with soil and tufts of grass were planted. The finished surface had an appearance closely resembling that of grassland. At low angles of

'Watson's Pots'—tufts of grass planted during the making of a concrete runway to conceal it (*Public Record Office*)

Concrete runway after grass from 'Watson's Pots' was fully grown
(*Public Record Office*)

vision the concrete was entirely hidden by blades of grass. This system was known as 'Watson's Pots' after Leslie Watson, a horticulturist member of the research section.

The arrival of the American Air Force was the reason for the expansion of many existing airfields and the construction of new ones. Concealment, such as it was, had to go by the board with the inevitable disfiguration of the landscape. All this evoked the criticism of the Inspector of Airfield Camouflage, Norman Wilkinson, who had held this post since the beginning of the war, the Admiralty being disenchanted with dazzle-painting.[8] Although an Honorary Air Commodore, Wilkinson found the number of committees he had to attend irksome and announced that airfield camouflage was largely a waste of time. Altogether about 32 million gallons of paint had been used for covering runways and buildings since September 1939 and Wilkinson thought it would be better to concentrate on a few vital airfields such as No 80 (Radio Countermeasures) Wing's base at Radlett and the Special Operations Executive base at Tempsford. He pointed out that during the Battle of Britain runways were repaired after an attack within a few hours.

Perhaps more important to the theory of camouflage was Wilkinson's discovery that patterned or disruptive painting was of limited value. At long range, disruption was reduced to one tone, while at closer range the patterning became obvious and advertised rather than concealed the target. The answer, believed Wilkinson, was to design for a mass disruptive effect at long range. Such views were to some extent confirmed in the official policy for camouflage at night. But they put him in bad odour with Turner who thought Wilkinson was interfering with policy and in 1942, on the pretext of age, Wilkinson was retired, his next official assignment being to paint the Normandy landings.

Camouflage of about 630 operational airfields continued until well into 1944 (there was always the threat of German intruder attacks). But less reliance was placed on paint and airfield buildings were often treated as part of a village or housing estate. Dummy aircraft were used to attract enemy bombs and the construction of dummy aircraft became so sophisticated that 'Spitfires' or 'Mustangs' could be rolled up and put into a bag, being erected when required.

Warships, particularly such capital ships as *King George V* and aircraft carriers, presented fine targets for enemy bombers when undergoing dock repair and unable to take evasive action.[9] In certain cases the sinking of a ship like *Tirpitz* could affect the balance of sea power. Docks are usually in the form of a basin and difficult to conceal. If one was camouflaged, nearby basins became more prominent. Massive structural camouflage with nets was not used by the British, not only because of the shortage of labour and cost of materials, but also because it was realised a strong shadow was cast by drapings from the high superstructure of a battleship. The favoured solution was to treat a big ship like a factory building and apply a disruptive design over it, breaking up the elliptical outline and merging the ship into her surroundings. New ships were to have camouflage paint applied as they took shape, instead of being launched with the smart grey beloved of the Admiralty.

Again, decoys were useful either in the form of lights, dummy hards, or dummy ships. This work was done by a static camouflage section at the Admiralty under Alan Durst, a sculptor who had executed important commissions for churches and Winchester Cathedral, assisted by John Nash, the landscape painter, both holding commissions in the Royal Marines. A number of their deceptions were successful: a laid-up merchantman in Plymouth harbour, disguised to look like the battleship *King George V*, was bombed, for example.

At night the glint of water provided valuable information for aircrew.[10] Reservoirs, lakes and estuaries leading to ports provided navigational aids or indicated the route to vital targets. In the former category were the reservoirs near Tottenham, Ruislip and Staines in the London area and the Welsh Harp in the West Midlands. In the second category there were the Stanton Mile reservoir near Northwood on the outskirts of London and Binley Lake near Coventry. When the Germans switched to night-bombing in the winter of 1940, making water surfaces less visible became increasingly important.

Tests were made from 1936 onwards at Hayling Island, Billingham and elsewhere with covering water surfaces with powdered coal or

Artificial lake of very pronounced shape—a landmark in the neighbourhood of vital factories

anthracite dust, but it was found to be impractical.[11] The film of dust was either blown to the windward shore or broken up by ripples. After spreading coal dust on the upper reaches of the Thames early in 1942, further attempts were abandoned. The most effective, though expensive, way of concealing water surface was to cover it with nets supported at some distance above the surface by a wire grid and carried by floats secured to a fixed anchorage ashore. Various forms of raft and float were devised. If the water was not providing an essential service, the lake or reservoir could be drained as was done in the case of a reservoir near Birmingham. Nature, in the course of time, completed the camouflage with a prolific growth of vegetation including willows no less than 8ft high.

After the lake had been drained a natural growth of vegetation covered the bed within eight months. Inset is a ground photograph of vegetation

Two plumes from cooling towers at Ham's Hall near Birmingham have been darkened. This was considered to be the most conspicuous industrial target in England

Other useful guides for the enemy were the plumes of steam and white smoke from cooling towers and chimneys. Smoke from the latter could be eliminated for short periods, but not steam plumes. Leon Underwood, with his proclivity for invention, was given the task of obscuring the cooling plant at Ham's Hall, considered the most conspicuous industrial target in the country. By burning pulverised pitch, the white steam was transformed to grey so that it merged into the dark tones of the surrounding landscape when seen from the air. Emissions from cement kilns were less easy to hide for when smoke was introduced it damaged the kiln lining and this practice had to be abandoned.[12]

Smoke itself was, of course, a means of obscuring industrial targets before the approach of hostile aircraft. A target could be covered in about fifteen to forty-five minutes. By day, smoke would attract the attention of aircrew and it was usually employed in the period before and after full moon. Before effective forms of smoke could be produced fundamental research was necessary, both at the Chemical Defence Research Establishment at Porton and the Fuel Research Station at Greenwich.[13] Smoke is a dispersion of solid or liquid particles in a gas. Working on this principle scientists, principally the physicist T. R. Merton, at that time a scientific adviser to the MAP, took as their starting point Rayleigh's proposition that light is scattered to a greater degree on a short rather than a long wavelength. This scattering was related to the size of the smoke particles and to the physical properties of the material from which the smoke was generated.

In Britain only two materials—oil and pitch—were available for smoke-screens. Oil generators mounted on lorries or trailers were developed by the Navy but the smoke did not last. Oil burners required a large labour force to keep them burning and a considerable amount of fuel. To produce 8 hours of smoke, 11 small oil burners were needed, burning 110 tons of fuel. Pitch gave out dense clouds of smoke but had a tendency to inflame. When water was thrown into the trough containing it, the smoke stopped and later flared up again (it was essential that there should be no glare or flame).

The next problem was to discover whether light or dark smoke was effective. After experiments, the best smoke seemed to lie between the two extremes, though light smoke was better in moonlight as its reflection factor was close to that of its background. Weather conditions had to be favourable. Winds with velocities greater than about 10mph caused the generators to flame and dispersed the smoke too quickly.

In spite of these problems, smoke-screens were used to cover industrial areas such as Coventry, Derby, Nottingham, Slough and ports and naval dockyards at Cardiff, Liverpool, Portsmouth and Chatham. Generators were lit when the bombers were 150 miles away and began to emit smoke when they were at a distance of 80 miles from the target. Up to April 1941, the intensive period of enemy air attacks on England, some 850 smoke-screens protected 28 vital points, none of which suffered damage from bombing during the smoke cover.

The Germans probably made more use of smoke to cover industrial areas as climatic conditions were more favourable than over England. Like the British, they experienced difficulties with materials and chemical smokes were largely used in the early part of the war; for example, the battleships *Scharnhorst* and *Gneisenau* were screened by chlorosulphonic acid while lying at Brest. But smoke-screens were not popular with factory workers, who said they had an effect like a combination of tear gas and sneezing powder. The Americans also devoted much scientific effort to smoke. They believed that white smoke made the best screen, though it reflected the light and therefore had to cover a much wider area than the target. Coloured smokes, on the other hand, blended into their surroundings and acted as a form of camouflage. Smoke discussed so far comes under the heading of strategical use. The tactical use of smoke in the various theatres of war will be considered in Chapters 5 and 6.

Did camouflage at all affect the accuracy of German night-bombing on British industrial targets? Detailed studies of the bombing of Britain were made by the Air Warfare Analysis Unit under the mathematician, Dr L. B. C. Cunningham.[14] They indicated that in area-bombing specific targets were not attacked. The height from which bombs were discharged during these raids varied from 8,000 to 15,000ft and seldom lower than 6,000ft, higher than the guide provided by the Camouflage Directorate. The average error of aim was around 400yd. Low-level attacks against specific targets were made from heights of 1,000ft and under and then presumably

camouflage was not so effective. Dive-bombing attacks were only
occasionally made on coastal areas and were not accurate. Experience
of bomber crews showed that camouflage seen directly from above
was irrelevant, as the target could be identified from adjacent land-
marks and it was unnecessary to observe the target during the run-up.
Flares were useful in identifying targets. By night, reflection from
large expanses of glass roof could be confusing especially when viewed
from an upmoon direction. Moderate use of texture to break up
shine from flat surfaces was all that was required. As already remarked, camouflage came into its own when radio navigational aids
broke down; and the primary concern of the design section at Leamington was to impede the visual recognition of *specific* targets.

It is possible that Turner's decoys were more useful than concealment.[15] Their purpose was to simulate by day or by night the
appearance of vital targets, with the object of diverting attack from
the real points. Turner himself believed that his fire-lighters had
effectively diverted enemy action, saving hundreds of lives and vital
war production. In the early days decoys, known as K sites, were used
to divert attacks from airfields. In August 1940 Turner organised
about 100 day and night dummy airfields and had erected about 400
dummy aircraft to attract the attention of enemy bombers. Decoys
(Q sites) had by then been provided for the principal aircraft factories
and they, too, drew bombs intended for the real target.[16] On 4 August,
for example, the decoy for Boulton & Paul, Wolverhampton, makers
of the Defiant two-seat fighter and power-operated gun turrets for
aircraft, was heavily bombed by three waves of aircraft. By night

Screens erected to conceal expanse of water which could provide a navigational
aid to an enemy bomber crew (*Public Record Office*)

small fires (QL sites) were intended to divert the raider from his target before he made an attack and were operated in the course of a raid by the parent factory or key point.

The Civil Defence Committee next approved the idea of decoys simulating marshalling yards and blast furnaces. An experimental site where train flashes, car lights and faulty black-out could be reproduced had already been set up under Curtis on the moors about five miles from the centre of Sheffield. The strength of the lighting was controlled by dimmers which could be regulated according to the weather conditions. On the basis of these experiments it was possible to go ahead with industrial decoys.

Russian camouflage of a water and oil tank truck beside a house
(*Public Record Office*)

Distinct from QL sites were town decoys, designed to protect the civil population rather than factories. They were called Starfish and were used increasingly after the German pathfinder unit *KG 100* used a radio beam to locate its target. After pathfinders had dropped flares, the main force unloaded its bombs in the illuminated area without identifying the target visually.

The Air Staff decided to increase Starfish on 23 November 1940 after the heavy raids on Coventry, Bristol, Birmingham and Southampton. The Treasury made a block grant of £2 million for this purpose. The Starfish at Bristol was the first in operation and in a heavy attack on the night of 2/3 December 1940 attracted 80 high-explosive bombs and caused no casualties to the civilian population. A repeat attack on the decoy was made four nights later. In due course another eighteen towns had Starfish installed near them, including

Sheffield, Birmingham, Derby and Crewe. Sites were usually located southwest, southeast and north of the town and five to ten miles from the centre. They were manned by detachments of twenty-five men from the RAF who, for one reason or another, were unfit for overseas service, and were commanded by a sergeant. They probably came under heavier fire than many of their comrades in 'active' theatres of war. Ultimate control for the lighting of the decoys lay with the headquarters of No 80 Wing, responsible for radio countermeasures and which was aware, through the deciphering of enemy signals by the Ultra machine, of the proposed target for attack. Starfish had their own telephone exchange, manually operated equipment relegated to store before the war by the Post Office after the installation of automatic equipment. The decoys would be lit after the pathfinders had dropped their bombs.

It was essential in order to maintain the maximum amount of deception that operation of the decoys should be closely related to enemy movements and change as the fire-raising tactics changed. From the technical point of view the ideal was to produce as much flame as possible with the minimum amount of combustible material. Turner discovered that when a small quantity of water was poured into a trough of fuel oil already burning fiercely (water having been separated into its basic elements), a series of small explosions and large bursts of flame rising up to 20 or 30ft occurred. He had an apparatus made by which it was possible to regulate the flow of water and simulate the effect of periodic bursts of flame like a burning building which emits bursts of flame as it collapses. On other occasions, braziers carrying slow-burning coal and other kinds of combustible material were used. With practice, techniques were improved, various kinds of fire being produced according to the weight of the enemy attack. At the end of the Blitz in the early summer of 1941, 140 Starfish sites were in operation. Most of them had closed down by the end of 1943, with the dying out of attacks on Britain by manned aircraft. But decoys continued to be operated during the campaigns in North Africa, Italy and north-west Europe.

The Germans also made considerable use of decoys to deflect the night attacks of RAF Bomber Command on area and industrial targets. During 1941–42 these decoys were similar to, though more elaborate than, those used by Col Turner's department. Usually they could be recognised on aerial photographs and a detailed record was built up by the photographic interpretation unit at Medmenham. Humphrey Spender, brother of the poet Stephen Spender, an architect who had turned to photography and painting, worked at Medmenham for much of the war. He recalls that a proper assessment of an apparently 'innocent' area was not always possible after it had been plastered with bombs and the evidence of a decoy destroyed.

German warship in dry dock camouflaged by matting and nets (*Public Record Office*)

German rocket launcher for launching rockets to simulate Bomber Command target indicators (*Public Record Office*)

German decoys consisted of groups of walled enclosures filled with combustible material which, when ignited, simulated the effect of a group of burning buildings. The sites were also identified on night photographs taken during a raid by the regular and close light tracks which they produced. But there were numerous occasions when they were successful in diverting a large part of the attack.[17] In the raid on Essen on 25/26 March 1942, for example, about 50 per cent of the photographs plotted were concentrated about twenty miles away from the target area and revealed decoy fires burning. This decoy site was not previously known, but its position was later confirmed by daylight photographic cover. There were many other instances of diversion of effort being caused by fire sites in 1942.

When Bomber Command introduced target-indicator bombs and sky-marking flares laid by the Pathfinder Group, aircraft no longer had to bomb on fires. In response to this change of tactics, the Germans devised decoy target indicators to burn both in the air and on the ground. In the former case they were simulated by large rockets fired from the ground. Decoy flares were also used. Deception against Bomber Command went on until the end of 1944 but with decreasing effect. There is no doubt that decoys helped limit the value of the British attacks, but the conclusion at the end of the war was that they had been most effective when the marking technique, for reasons of weather or technical failure, had not gone according to plan. Their effect on major operations was usually negligible as time went on. This was the result of the improved skill of the Pathfinder crews, the direction of operations by a master bomber, the fact that the target

Structural camouflage of Rheinania Ossag oil refinery. Oil targets became top priority for the Allied bombers in 1944 (*Public Record Office*)

Camouflaged oil tanks, Bonn (*Public Record Office*)

indicators were a poor imitation of the British ones, and, finally, the thorough briefing of bomber crews in what kind of decoys to expect.

German camouflage fell into two categories.[18] First, there were permanent schemes, often begun before the war, in which great shelters were built over ground in cities to resemble buildings and covered either by turf or by dummy structures. Sometimes castellations were added including, in one case, a tower complete with weather vane and cock. Secondly, there were schemes for concealing such vital key points as oil refineries, aircraft and munition factories. Such schemes were very elaborate compared with British ones and structural materials rather than paint were used. A typical example was the synthetic rubber plant at Hüls in the Ruhr. It was largely covered with wire-netting, interwoven with tufts of glass wool. The colours were repainted to match the season. Around one part, small trees of wood, wire and glass wool were erected, the whole scheme costing about 4 million Reichmarks.

Despite this lavish treatment it was a failure: the wire-netting rusted, sections were blown down, and it was impossible to find paint that stuck to the glass wool. Men badly needed to work at the bench were permanently employed in maintaining it. Furthermore it failed to deceive either the aerial camera or divert the bomber. An elaborate decoy was built about three miles away from the main plant, complete with streets, dummy buildings, cooling towers and gas holders. It was so realistic that the managing director once thought he was in the real plant. But it did not attract a single bomb throughout the war.

British and American teams later investigated the effects of the bomber offensive and Thomas and Ironside from Leamington compared the enemy camouflage with their own designs.[19] (As civilians, the battledress they had to wear overseas carried an arm band with the letters SD (Special Duty) and, on landing in France, had hastily to be removed as it was interpreted as Sicherheit Dienst, or Gestapo!) They found that the Germans had been ingenious in the use of materials for netting, though less imaginative in application. Fibre had been replaced by wire-netting garnished with a combination of natural and artificial materials such as twigs and rags and coarse paper. This covering was strong and resilient and, apart from the twigs, reasonably inflammable. Plastic sheeting was also used and green dye to colour brushwood. Concrete surfaces were sometimes mottled in green, grey, black or tan paint.

What distinguished German camouflage from that of the Allies was the magnitude of their schemes made possible by the quantity of forced labour. Large areas of water were made to resemble land, including 30,000 acres of Lake Maesche near Hannover and an area twice as big over the Binner Alster in Hamburg, the latter being destroyed in the great incendiary raids of 1943. Vast platforms were constructed, over which was laid a mat of rushes, branches and coarse netting. Imitation hills were added 15ft high. Clusters of lath framework covered with nets were painted to imitate trees and bushes.

Better co-ordination and supervision, as was practised by agencies such as the Camouflage Committee in Britain, would have averted some of the German excesses like the dummy windows and even letter boxes seen on some buildings. However, the construction of elaborate decoys as at Hamburg had to be done in daylight and so was photographed. It was, indeed, the constant coverage by British photographic reconnaissance aircraft and the skilled interpretation of the photographs that defeated the German camouflage effort. Without early cover of any suspect activity, Spender has remarked, it was never safe to jump to any conclusions about camouflage.

Apart from that, pin-point bombing, which industrial camouflage was intended to delay or divert, was rarely attempted visually (the precision attacks on oil refineries in 1944–5 were always made on radar). The American heavy bombers employed in the daylight offensive usually operated at heights of 27,000 to 30,000ft using semi- or fully automatic bombsights. The target was a 'circle having a radius of 1,000ft round the aiming point' and it was reckoned that 'only about one bomb in five fell within the target'.

In addition to smoke-screens, always subject to the vagaries of the weather, apart from being indicative of the target, the Germans tried to confuse bomber pilots by turning powerful arc searchlights on them. The glare was intensified by large mirrors often 80in wide. But again the effort involved was not commensurate with the results obtained.

5 FROM PASSIVE TO OFFENSIVE

> Dummy equipment is part of the normal equipment of war and is
> used by both sides in most operations, either to distract the
> enemy's attention or to misrepresent intention.
>   General Headquarters, Home Forces, 14 December 1943

To say that the Guards Brigade was responsible for reviving camouflage in the British Army before World War II might cause anyone
who knew that unit's reputation for spit and polish to smile. In 1936
Brig A. (later Sir Andrew) Thorne took over command of the 1st
Guards Brigade. Thorne had just returned from Berlin where he had
been military attaché; he had attended German army manoeuvres
and noted the importance attached to concealment from the air, track
discipline, fieldcraft, the camouflaged ground-sheets with which the
infantry were equipped and the trucks painted in green, ochre and
brown.[1] Thorne was a friend of Capt Liddell Hart, the military critic,
and held similar views on the urgent need to modernise the Army.

In the summer of that year Thorne's brigade tested various kinds
of camouflage on two exercises around Aldershot in collaboration with
RAE, Farnborough. Gerald Palmer of the Chemical Department,
which had been working on designs for aircraft and airfield camouflage, provided colour designs for vehicles, based on models in grey,
ochre and green. Aircraft from the nearby RAF School of Air Photography tested the effectiveness of garnished netting and painted sheets
for eliminating shadows from vehicles. Using brigade funds, Thorne
purchased pea-netting and even garden parasols to hide his headquarters and to simulate a dummy one. Gen Wavell, who had served
on Allenby's staff in Palestine and was addicted to deception, was an
interested spectator of these schemes.

Shortly after, the brigade was sent to Palestine to keep the peace
between Jew and Arab, and where the camouflage schemes were put
into use, but not before Thorne had written a valuable report sum-
marising the results of the exercises he had initiated. This bore fruit
in the following spring when the War Office decided to introduce
camouflage on a large scale, starting with the disruptive painting of
vehicles, while experiments were to be continued with various types
of netting.

This work was supervised by the Royal Engineer and Signals
Board, responsible for the provision of technical equipment, and at
the outbreak of war two sapper majors were busily engaged in
preparing camouflage designs for various types of military installation.

Frederick, brother of Jack Beddington, the well-known director of publicity for Shell-Mex and BP, who as a young officer on the Western Front was equipped with one of the few rifles fitted with telescopic sights, had, of necessity, developed an interest in the art of concealment and now offered his services to the War Office. He was eagerly accepted by the hard-pressed subcommittee for camouflage as a civilian assistant.

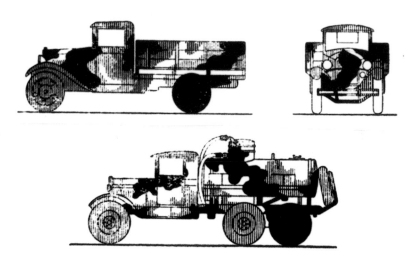

Mechanisation of armies in the 1930s led to disruptive painting of vehicles. Drawings from a Russian manual (*Public Record Office*)

As the British Expeditionary Force in France had no camouflage organisation, Beddington, to his astonishment, was appointed camouflage adviser to the engineer-in-chief, there being no other person suitable for the job.[2] After serving briefly as a major at general headquarters, he was promoted to lieutenant-colonel, and in company with a sculptor, also in uniform, formed what was officially designated the Camouflage Experimental Section. Its function, largely unfulfilled, was to try out new devices and materials, such as steel wool, prepare working specifications and drawings to be produced either at home or at a camouflage factory set up near Rouen, and to hold courses and organise demonstrations for commanders and staff. Beddington had a small aircraft at his disposal from which to view the defences, and his reputation—and by inference the stock of camouflage in general— soared high in the eyes of his brother officers when he was able to deliver a load of fresh fish from Dieppe to enliven the austere diet preferred by the spartan commander-in-chief, Lord Gort.

The camouflage factory was in charge of a sapper captain and temporarily numbered among its staff, Alec Waugh, the writer, and an ATS officer. It was modelled on a World War I pattern and employed local female labour to garnish nets, though it was also

Officer and men on patrol. Dummy figures displayed by the Camouflage Development and Training Centre, Farnham (*Imperial War Museum*)

intended to produce dummy equipment, and one of its projected assignments was to design dummy tanks capable of being folded up, to be used either in an actual attack, or to simulate a concentration of armoured vehicles.[3]

These activities were abruptly halted by the German breakthrough in May 1940 and Beddington, assisted by Godfrey Money Coutts, incinerated in a brewer's vat on the road to Dunkirk the voluminous files and drawings compiled by the engineer-in-chief's staff during the past months. The Home Forces now had to prepare to meet an invasion with totally inadequate equipment. Concealment and deception were never more necessary to cover the Army's deficiencies, but there was no one to preach the gospel. The War Office therefore set up a Camouflage Development and Training Centre (CDTC), Beddington being instrumental in selecting the ideal site at Farnham Castle, then belonging to the Bishop of Winchester, whose numerous apartments had housed some 30 clergymen in retreat until recently. The cedar-shaded grounds could be used for demonstrations and Farnborough airfield was at hand to accustom officers to flying. Jack Beddington, now director of the Films Division in the Ministry of Information, because of his knowledge of the art world, proved to be of great assistance to his brother, who became the first commandant, by helping him to judge the potentialities of would-be camoufleurs—there were at least 300 candidates to fill 30 vacancies and not every artist could be tolerated within the military hierarchy. Frederick Beddington was later appointed inspector of camouflage to the Home Forces, and in that capacity represented the Army on the Camouflage Committee at Leamington until 1942.

The chief instructor at Farnham was Col Richard Buckley MC, who had served under Wyatt on the Western Front. Despite an abrupt manner, his clear thinking and enthusiasm inspired even the most unmilitary of the successive cadres of painters, designers and architects who passed through the centre, becoming staff officers (camouflage) attached to army or corps headquarters and who, in due course, were posted to the Mediterranean or Far-Eastern theatres of war. The artists ranged from the avant-garde to the traditional and included the painters Blair Hughes-Stanton, Edward Seago, Frederick Gore and Julian Trevelyan, who since his experience in civil camouflage had been approved for a commission by Buckley, and the designers Steven Sykes and Ashley Havinden. Others connected with the arts were Gabriel White, later a pillar of the Arts Council and Fred Mayor, who decorated the rooms with Rouaults and Matisses and other modern masters from his London gallery. The effect the artists had on officers transferred to camouflage from regular units was often startling. Garbed in unfamiliar battledress, they would clatter down the oak stairs of the castle in their new boots and perform rudimentary drill before embarking on the round of lectures, discussions and the practical work of erecting camouflage nets and playing

Large nets erected to conceal stores in open country (*Imperial War Museum*)

hide-and-seek in sniper's suits. Trevelyan later recalled the feeling of returning to school induced by the outdoor exercise and stale class-room smell. He shared an attic bedroom with a New Zealander who sat up in bed knitting socks until the lights were turned out.[4]

But at Farnham there were some compensations of a more civilised nature, including a well-stocked cellar which nearly terminated the life of a rather elderly visiting lecturer. He came back late one night after talking to the troops and, having refreshed himself, fell asleep on a sofa with a lighted cigarette. Not long after he was rescued by brother officers awakened by the pungent smell of burning fabric. As this was a camouflage unit, no court of enquiry was held on the cause of the fire in the mess!

Not all the camoufleurs had an artistic background. There was the conjurer Jasper Maskelyne who, on account of recent events, had just had an unsatisfactory season at the seaside resorts he usually frequented; and there was Hugh Cott, frustrated in trying to propa-gate the principles of natural camouflage in Whitehall, who now had to master elementary tactics and learn how to identify targets from fast-flying aircraft.

The corps into which these men of such diverse talents were com-missioned was usually the Royal Engineers. But there was one exception, Roland Penrose, doyen of the pre-war English Surrealists, and at the time a civilian lecturer to the Home Guard. His system of teaching was indeed partly derived from Surrealism. In order to demonstrate how conspicuous the slightest movement is when seen from the air he would place a button in a piece of grass around which he assembled his audience. He then tugged at the thread to which the button was attached, immediately drawing everyone's attention to it. The greater part of the work of those trained at the CDTC was, in fact, to make troops visually aware of their surroundings and how to merge themselves into it. And this was done not only by demonstrations but by training pamphlets and posters produced by the centre. Intelligence summaries were issued indicating how they might recognise the enemy's camouflage techniques. On the develop-ment side the centre conducted experiments in new methods and advised on the construction and use of equipment.

Such advice was sorely needed, for after Dunkirk the well-inten-tioned attempts to transform pill-boxes into public lavatories, chicken houses, or romantic ruins, while sometimes effective, were more often likely to draw attention to their presence. Oliver Messel, the elegant designer and decorator whose last commission before the outbreak of war had been to decorate the Royal Box at Covent Garden, was one of those who fulfilled themselves by conjuring up the most improbable disguises for these pentagonal objects.

It was the camouflage net which, as in World War I, was probably the most useful item of equipment and was carried, already garnished, by artillery, tanks and transport vehicles. The gunners were equipped with fish-netting garnished with 2in-wide strips of scrim, forming an irregular patch inside the square of the net; its thinned-out edge was intended to avoid a sharp cast shadow. Sometimes the scrim was tied in bows to increase the effect of texture. In other types of net the irregular patch was formed by sewing on pea-bagging or coir, or even rags stained with sump oil. Vehicle-netting could be used to simulate the locality of the parking place; outhouses if parked by buildings, or bushes if sited alongside trees or hedgerows. Tanks were equipped with shrimp-netting, the small mesh preventing projections on the surfaces becoming entangled.

Concealment was usually designed as protection against the low oblique view, either of an observer or camera. Primarily, defended localities depended on how they were sited and this was done by making the best use of available cover. But often artificial materials were required. The CDTC devised a variety of aids including cover for machine-gun posts, mats of painted hessian or coir-netting to hide newly excavated spoil, screens to conceal gun flash or troop movements and overhead covers for vehicles which could be slung from trees or thrown over frames made from hop poles. Experiments with types of netting were made to find the lightest, most resistant to rough handling, able to stand up to bad weather and decay and unlikely to lose colour. Other qualities were non-inflammability and ability to soften shadows. Towards the end of 1943, Buckley was able to claim that the nets they had devised had kept down casualties and preserved equipment, provided they were used properly. Even in the Tunisian sun and rain they kept their colour.[5]

The concealment of guns in mobile warfare was always a difficult problem. However well-painted, barrels were conspicuous and the distinctive rectangular shape of the shield and the movements of the gun crew behind it all combined to attract attention. The CDTC invented a 'gun cosy' made of dark and textured material with bunched garnish to eliminate shine and the sides of the gun covered with screens. The irregular outline so formed distorted the shape of the shield and helped to conceal the crew, provided that the camouflage of the equipment was related to the background. This imaginative approach was characteristic of British Army camouflage, whereas the Germans confined themselves to improvising and making use of local materials.

The camouflage of such military installations as dumps, oil tanks and coastal batteries, and other static targets, was the concern of a section known as Royal Engineers 8 (RE8) in the Ministry of Supply. It liaised closely with Leamington, sharing as it did similar interests. The enemy's growing appreciation from the end of 1940 onwards of

'Gun cosy'. Camouflaged shield and barrel of 25 pounder field gun
(*Imperial War Museum*)

Britain's superiority in radar was the reason for greater attention to the camouflage of radar stations. This was done by a section in the Air Ministry called Works War (WW). Apart from a few attacks during the Battle of Britain, they had, surprisingly enough, not attracted the attention of enemy bombers. The high towers of the Home Chain stations and the buildings housing generators, radio and other equipment, which for technical reasons had to be sited close by, did not make the task of the camoufleur in WW easy.[6] From then onwards, however inconvenient, buildings were more widely dispersed and the most important of them were well hidden; dummy buildings were erected and false tracks laid to distract the bomb-aimer's attention. Masts and towers were staggered, instead of being sited in a straight line and the shape of the towers broken by bands of paint in varying depths of tone. Technical advice in static camouflage such as this was provided by the engineer-in-chief's staff at the War Office.

As the danger of invasion receded, planning for more aggressive forms of warfare took precedence and greater attention was paid to deception. The fighting in the Western Desert had shown what an important part camouflage could play, provided it was directed from the highest level. From the autumn of 1942, no less an officer than the Director of Military Operations—then Maj-Gen J. N. Kennedy—at the War Office, became responsible for camouflage and deception and a directorate was formed for special weapons and vehicles, dealing with the production and distribution of special devices, including dummy equipment, smoke and sonic warfare. In a short while it attracted several desert officers, who had made camouflage work and knew what was required. Another was Victor Stiebel, the fashion designer, who supervised the despatch of camouflage officers to various theatres of war.

At the same time Richard Buckley at Farnham continued to do much of the creative thinking and at the courses run for officers and NCOs he and his staff opened the eyes of the Army to the possibilities of surprise. Trevelyan believed that Buckley 'saved the sort of wasted effort to which the Germans were at that time so prone; for many of the grandiose camouflage schemes never succeeded in deflecting a single bomb.'[7] An important feature of the Farnham courses was the display of models organised by the designer, Charles Gardiner.

Aural deception or sonic warfare, as it was known, practised in various forms since Joshua instructed the children of Israel to shout before the walls of Jericho, could now with the aid of recording equipment and loudspeakers mounted on a small cross-country vehicle produce an effect out of all proportion to the men and equipment involved. Lt-Col C. D. Barlow, at that time serving in the Colonial Office, was responsible for introducing the idea and in a few months was training the first sonic warfare units in a remote part of Ayrshire in Scotland.[8] His proposal was that small armoured scout cars manned by hand-picked signallers and Tank Corps drivers would penetrate to within 1,000yd or so of the enemy and reproduce sounds of tanks, vehicles, or automatic weapons.

The deception would, of course, be linked to the plan of operations, the object usually being to distract attention from another part of the battlefield. The formation and training of under a dozen light scout-car companies was highly secret and not until the end of 1943 were commanders-in-chief allowed to use them at their own discretion. Wavell, who had submitted a paper to the War Office on the subject before the war, was one of the first to ask for two units to be sent to India, where in the jungle fighting the Japanese, noise was more likely to create an effect than in European and Mediterranean battlefields.

Sonic devices were also introduced into seaborne assault landings, the first occasion being the landings in Sicily. The deception was then on a small scale, but as the technique of combined operations was developed along the coast of Italy, reaching its peak in 1944, tactical deception allied to a grand strategic deception scheme involving a number of media, became ever more sophisticated in application. Once the Americans had appreciated that sonic warfare was not simply a matter of making a big bang, they also exploited their wealth of radio equipment and technical expertise in operations of this nature.

By the late summer of 1943 south and south-east England was becoming a vast military camp as it filled up with troops concentrating for the invasion of Europe—Operation 'Overlord'. Although Fighter Command had established superiority in the air, it was impossible to prevent the occasional high-altitude photo-reconnaissance or bombing aircraft from crossing the coast. Concealment against a bomber involved the use of patterning as opposed to the general darkening required to deceive the photographic interpreter. As elaborate camouflage was more likely than not to give away a target on a photograph, troops were instructed to camouflage against high-altitude photography. It was assumed that the enemy would be unlikely to photograph the whole area so that a camp, for instance, which failed to catch an observer's eye could well escape being photographed. Top priority for camouflage was not given to hutted camps of a semi-permanent nature, but to tented camps containing 2,000 troops or less, which for tactical or strategic reasons should not attract attention. In Southern Command, where the bulk of the British Overlord forces was assembling, it was reckoned that no more than about 5 per cent could be concealed.

Seago, the East Anglian landscape artist, was in charge of camouflage here and operated from the headquarters at Wilton House, home of the Earl of Pembroke. Two of his commanders-in-chief—Auchinleck and Alexander—were keen amateur artists and found Seago congenial company. His approach to camouflage evolved from the impractical—nets covered with horse hair to hide Dorset beach defences and life-sized models, ordered from a London film studio, of Neville Chamberlain clad in battledress and steel helmet, each mounted on a turntable with a rifle fixed at a different angle, to man dummy gun pits—to simple schemes requiring the minimum use of materials and labour. In this vein Seago issued instructions that it was a waste of time to camouflage sites near conspicuous features. On specific points of detail he advised that spoil showing through thin cover should be darkened, using local materials such as clinkers, huts should be darkened by paint, and smokeless cooking apparatus employed. Troops should not move into wooded areas, of which there were an abundance in Hampshire and Dorset, until the trees were in leaf.

In the months before D-day, the units destined to cross the Channel took part in innumerable exercises which involved embarking on landing craft, making practice attacks on beaches, returning to port and disembarking. These activities, which took place at various points along the south coast, could, and were, used to deceive the enemy.[10] Troops often embarked at night and a deception plan was arranged by Colonel Turner, that master of decoy, in which the hards to be used for the invasion were to be lit up regularly for about five months before D-day in order to accustom the enemy to seeing them, so that when the actual date came he would be less likely to take interest. At the same time, decoy hards were to be lit at sporadic intervals. In south-east England, from which the enemy was intended to believe that the main assault would be launched, ports and embarkation areas would be illuminated frequently.

Meantime the American armies were assembling in south-west England. Compared with the British, the American camoufleurs were combat soldiers as well as specialists. They were organised into battalions, consisting of 30 officers and some 400 men with one attached to each army. A battalion was subdivided into four companies, each of which was allotted to a corps. They, in turn, were divided into four platoons of one officer and a dozen men, who advised on the concealment problems of a division. A factory unit at GHQ was responsible for providing materials. Six camouflage battalions accompanied the American forces to Europe.

The driving force behind American Army camouflage was Lt-Col Homer Saint-Gaudens who, it will be recalled, had notably assisted in instilling the notion in American troops in World War I. He had, in the meantime, become Director of Fine Arts at the Carnegie Institute, Pittsburgh, one of his duties being to organise the annual international exhibitions of painting sponsored by the institute. This involved travelling to Europe, and Saint-Gaudens took the opportunity to keep in touch with camouflage developments, attending manoeuvres in Germany and discovering that current British ideas about camouflage differed little in principle from those of the Americans.

In 1940 he was one of several officers in the engineer-in-chief's office responsible for reviving camouflage and later imparting instruction to the new armies formed when America entered the war. Much of the experimental work took place at Fort Belvoir, Virginia, an establishment similar to Farnham, but equipment in desert and snow conditions was tested at Indio, California, and on the 14,000ft-high slopes of Mount Rainier in the northwest. Saint-Gaudens believed that camouflage was both a science (with a plumber's kit) and an art and in choosing potential camouflage officers he liked to have architects 'who knew how to design linen closets and stairways in the same place'. Hollywood property men were another useful source for practical ideas. Saint-Gaudens accompanied the American forces to Britain and supervised the concealment of their activities in Devon and Cornwall before D-day. Concealment in the latter county was less easy than in the leafy coombs of Devon but, with track discipline and the netting of tentage in parallel lines to ditches and hedges, much could be hidden from high-level photographic reconnaissance.

Long before the invasion plans were completed, and the forces trained, agents were being dropped or landed in enemy-occupied territory to carry out sabotage and other kinds of subversive operations. Responsibility for their organisation and despatch lay with the celebrated Special Operations Executive (SOE) about which there has been a wealth of literature, much of it inaccurate and misleading. Although SOE was formed soon after the withdrawal from the Continent, it was not until the spring of 1941 that agents began to arrive and only in the summer of 1942 were their activities on an appreciable scale.

In November 1941, SOE (or SO2 as it was then known) engaged a camouflage expert to advise on various methods of concealing devices which might be used by agents infiltrating into France and other countries.[11] Such advice was soon found to be inadequate so in January 1942 a small workshop operated by a staff of three began to carry out experimental work. Very shortly this group, designated Section XV, expanded into a full-scale camouflage section. Its headquarters was located in a road house on the Barnet bypass near Elstree. Experimental work on prototypes and demonstrations went on in several rooms behind the Victorian Gothic façade of the Natural History Museum and it was here that the King, fascinated by what he was shown, spent a lengthy visit towards the end of the war. Photographic and make-up work was done in offices in Trevor Square. Eventually, 18 officers and nearly 300 other ranks, including carpenters, metal workers, painters, plasterers and textile workers, were engaged in the production of 'properties' of one kind or another. As SOE's activities spread to other theatres of war, camouflage sections were set up in Cairo, Algiers and Italy, and, to support clandestine operations in Japanese-occupied territory, similar sections were formed in India and Australia.

A number of original devices were produced by Station XV. The first was a lipstick-holder, concealing a small message to be taken abroad by a woman agent. Wooden sabots were made, the soles of which were filled with plastic explosives and a time delay required for a sabotage operation. Glass floats of fishing nets were drilled and the insides painted with a fluorescent substance to act as night markers to indicate where watertight containers filled with explosives, arms and ammunition had been placed under the sea by SOE fishing boats near the French coast, later to be picked up by members of the Resistance in their own boats. In the compositors' and printing section, labels in foreign languages were exactly copied so that when the time came they could be stuck on suitcases, or food labels fixed to tins containing explosives. Incendiary devices with safety switches were attached to briefcases and other carriers so that, should they be opened by an unauthorised person, the contents were burned. Explosives were naturally an important item and were tested in a special compound. They included bizarre items such as plastic explosives resembling coal, explosives concealed inside logs of wood used by saboteurs to drop into coal- or wood-fired boilers, and tyre bursters camouflaged to look like horse or cow dung.

As most operators were dropped by parachute, the size and weight of the devices made in the workshops often presented problems. Millions of notes in foreign currencies needed for operational purposes overseas were concealed in different kinds of carriers. Agents' clothing had to resemble exactly the products of the country in which their

Command post at Margival near Soissons built for Hitler to direct the invasion of Britain and where in June 1944 he was told by von Rundstedt of the difficulties being experienced under overwhelming Allied air superiority
(*Public Record Office*)

wearers were going to operate. Thus camouflage in special operations could literally be a matter of life or death.

The Normandy landings are recognised to be a masterpiece of combined-operational planning. Camouflage and deception were integral parts of the plan. The preparations could not be concealed from the enemy, but it was essential to deceive him as to the time, weight and direction of attack. A deception plan should induce the enemy commander-in-chief to make the wrong deductions from the information he received from ground and air sources.

From the Allied point of view, a rapid build-up ashore had to be achieved before the arrival of the German main reserves. It was here that deception could play an important part, for von Rundstedt, the German commander-in-chief, would be unlikely to commit his armoured reserves until he was quite sure which was the main Allied effort. Known as 'Fortitude', the deception plan was intended to make the Germans deduce that the main assault would take place against the Pas de Calais, this being the shortest sea route over which continuous air cover could be maintained, and a force established on the far shore could in a short while reach the Ruhr and the heart of Germany. In the Pas de Calais lay the German 15th Army, capable of switching formations to Normandy once it was known that it was the main area of attack; and it could quickly reinforce divisions trying to stem Allied encroachments inland.

'Fortitude' contained not only visual but radio and radar deception operations which began to take effect some months before D-day.[12] Both sides accepted interception of radio traffic as inevitable and it provided an excellent medium by which the enemy could be led to build up a false order of battle and to plot false dispositions. It became possible to give the impression that Montgomery's headquarters, which was outside Portsmouth, was in the Kent area south-east of London, by carrying its radio signals by land line to Kent and then transmitting them from there. Radio was also used to convey the idea that the 1st Canadian and 3rd American Armies intended to follow up the assault force were, in fact, concentrating in south-east England, preparatory to landing in the Pas de Calais. The Germans were encouraged to believe that this army group was led by Lt-Gen George S. Patton, well known as an aggressive commander and also senior to Gen Omar Bradley, the real commander of the American invasion force.

Both these subterfuges depended for success on good intelligence work by the German staff and it was assumed that they would make logical deductions; but in the case of the Japanese it will be shown that sophisticated deception plans rarely worked because their intelligence work was of poor quality and Japanese commanders obstinately refused to change their plans because of intelligence warnings. On the whole the 'correct' responses were made by the Germans before the landings and although Allied intelligence had some anxious moments when Normandy *was* reinforced, there were no reductions of strength in the Pas de Calais, even for some time *after* the assault to the west had taken place.

The visual plan of deception was designed to display both air and sea concentrations.[13] The former were comparatively easy to mount and took the form of dummy gliders assembling on airfields in Kent and East Anglia.

Construction and siting of dummy landing craft demanded more ingenuity, men and materials. They had already been used on a small scale in North Africa, but the idea for their large-scale deployment in English ports and estuaries came from Col Turner's brain early in 1943 and it shortly became an important stage of 'Fortitude'. Plans were drawn up for two types of dummy landing craft. Dummy Landing Craft Tank (LCTs) were known as Big Bobs and were 160ft long and 30ft wide at the maximum beam, built with light metal tubing and covered over with canvas lashed to the framework. This structure floated on 40-gallon petrol drums and the realism was heightened by anchors, bollards and coils of rope simulated by patches on camouflage nets. Each Big Bob required six 3-ton lorries to carry it to the coast and assembly, done at night, took about six hours.

Wet Bobs, representing Landing Craft Assault (LCAs), were much smaller in size and consisted of a canvas cover, short and long struts and an inflatable device; they were stowed away in two packets and twenty-four 'craft' could be carried in a 3-ton lorry.

The plan was that 255 Big Bobs were to be erected and launched by men of the 4th Northants and 10th Worcesters at Great Yarmouth, Lowestoft, Dover, Folkestone and in the estuaries of the Deben and

Orwell. Naval personnel 'operated' the craft once on the water. About 138 Wet Bobs were to be inflated and moored in similar areas. Both types of craft were intended to deceive photographers operating at high or vertical level, rather than from low-level oblique or from close ground or sea observation. Care had to be taken to conceal the assembly area as a normal stores dump and recognisable nautical equipment was well hidden. For this reason the flotation drums were not incorporated until the last moment. The flotillas were anchored for two weeks before and after D-day to give the impression that the attack west of the Seine was a feint.

The radio-decoy aspects of 'Fortitude' fall outside the limits of this study of visual deception. Suffice it to say that a mock invasion against the Pas de Calais was mounted by a few aircraft dropping Window—strips of tin foil normally used to jam the German ground radar on the approach of a bombing force. The aircraft flew according to pre-arranged patterns, approaching the enemy coast at the speed of a convoy of ships. In order to increase the illusion of approaching vessels, the bundles of Window were adjusted in size so that there was a variation in the echo received by the German sets. This strategic diversion was timed to take place as the real assault force was sailing towards the Normandy coast.

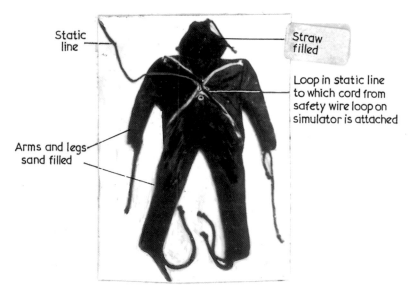

Type of dummy parachutist dropped over Normandy on the night before D-day
(*Public Record Office*)

In order to provide a distraction for the airborne landings (airborne troops being vulnerable to attack while they are forming up after the drop), a large-scale diversion was arranged to take place in the area south-west of Caen. Dummy paratroops made of sandbags, one-third the normal size of a man with parachutes to the same scale, were dropped by No 3 Group, Bomber Command. Attached to them were noise simulators which, when the dummies had struck the ground, exploded to represent rifle, mortar and machine-gun fire. Further realism was added by the release of pin-tail bombs from the aircraft. They discharged a Very light after touching the ground, the object being to advertise the area of the dummy drop and to give the impression that a reception party on the ground was signalling to the dummy-dropping aircraft. In the air the movement of large forces was created by the dropping of Window. Altogether some 500 dummies, provided by the Directorate of Special Weapons and Vehicles, were dropped and further confusion was induced among the enemy by the dropping of a small number of Special Air Service troops who were *real*. As it happened, the widely scattered drop of the American airborne troops mystified the Germans still further.

As soon as the Allied armies were firmly established on the far shore and had begun to drive towards the German frontier, logistics became as important as strategy and tactics. The voracious requirements of a mechanised army were anticipated by the laying of pipelines under the Channel (PLUTO), first to Cherbourg and then to Boulogne. Although precautions had to be taken to ensure that land and sea lines were inconspicuous, the terminals containing reciprocating and centrifugal pumps were extremely vulnerable.

Several camouflage officers from CDTC, including Ashley Havinden, industrial artist and textile designer, and the graphic artist Reg Lander were attached to the Petroleum Warfare Department and given the task of concealing the terminals situated on the south coast near Dungeness and at Shanklin on the Isle of Wight.[14] The latter was most important to conceal as it was to supply petrol to Cherbourg and, if located by the enemy, would give an important clue as to where the landings would take place. The main consideration was to preserve the appearance of the sites as they were before installation of the pumping system and no signs of their construction could be permitted. Concealment had to be most thorough including photography and observation from every angle.

The first step was to take a number of oblique and vertical aerial photographs of the proposed pumping sites and surroundings. They were chosen with a view to causing as little change as possible from their normal state and at Shanklin they included a derelict fort and adjacent mound, a hotel and garages, a golf clubhouse, an ice-cream factory and a number of bombed or derelict buildings on the esplanade. In certain cases, concrete walls and roofs had to be constructed and were carefully treated with gravel, rubble and clinker so as to blend with the broken and deserted appearance of the houses. Concrete was also cantilevered out on edges of buildings in an irregu-

PLUTO terminal at Shanklin, Isle of Wight. View of reconstructed mound from fort (*Imperial War Museum*)

lar pattern to break up the square outline of the new structures from air photography. The mound of the fort was partially excavated to accommodate several pumps and a switch house and was afterwards remoulded by turfing and by laying steel wool attached to XPM (expanded metal) which was supported by tubular scaffolding bent to shape and designed to simulate a gentle slope. Pipelines and cables entering the area were not always easy to conceal as field boundaries could not always be followed. This problem was overcome by ploughing allotment patches to measure and where possible carrying pipes along the existing tracks or footpaths and through bomb debris, the rubble being carefully raked over after the pipes had been laid. Filter pits had to be covered and sufficient space allowed for men to operate the valves beneath. Irregular open-ended covers resembling a rounded hut were made and were covered with steel wool and although not entirely invisible from the air were at least inconspicuous. Spoil from trenches running from the pumps to the filter pits was covered over with clinker, the whole road being taken up when this was being done to give the impression that road work was in progress. Finally, groynes on the beach were used to shield pipelines as they ran into the water.

Concrete mixers and other equipment were brought to the site at night and the workforce of some 300 men was lectured on camouflage and track discipline to get them to use existing roads, paths and tracks, the less obvious ones being wired in to prevent anyone straying from them. This warning was at once appreciated by the men and a small squad spent its time sweeping away mess from roads which might reveal what was afoot. All construction materials were covered with netting, and derelict buildings housed machinery and enabled welding and other operations to take place under cover.

So thorough were these precautions that the enemy never interfered with pumping operations, which began three months after D-day and continued until the German surrender. The pipelines were extended into Holland and Germany as the armies advanced, and by 1945 over a million gallons a day were being pumped across the Channel, saving tankers badly needed in other theatres of war.

As the Luftwaffe, handicapped by lack of pilots and fuel, was unable to challenge the Allied tactical air forces, camouflage in Europe largely went by the board. Indeed, it became necessary to make Allied vehicles more distinctive. They were painted with a five-pointed star so that when travelling in convoy, or otherwise could not be concealed, were easily identified by friendly aircraft. Thus the fortunes of war were reversed for in 1940 the Germans advancing into France draped their vehicles with swastika flags to ensure recognition from the air.

Once across the Channel American camouflage, like that of the British, became as Saint-Gaudens later wrote 'a matter of secondary importance' not only in the air but often from observation on the ground as the Germans had little or no ammunition to spare for counter-battery fire or shelling of rear areas. Only when units came under fire was trouble taken to conceal and the lessons learnt in training were hastily applied. After the break-out from Normandy the Americans took over the German camouflage factory in Paris. Here materials were produced for the hiding of pumping stations and tank farms sited alongside the pipelines developed from PLUTO. Fuel dumps were one type of target that the enemy did attempt to bomb but they were usually so well hidden that little damage was caused. No attempt, on the other hand, was made in the early days of the campaign to conceal airfields, many of which had been rapidly constructed by the engineers and where because of the 'mud and dust and stress of war' concealment was virtually impossible. But when airfields were located in the Low Countries within easy range of German fighter-bombers, some of which were jet-propelled, the cry went up for camouflage and netting and dummies were brought up under the supervision of Col Turner, who had extended his decoy operations into the battle area.

Heavy falls of snow during the battle of the Ardennes, in which the Americans took the major part, found the troops unprepared but white parkas were issued to forward units and trucks were hastily given a coat of whitewash. Unfortunately the lesson learnt on Mount Rainier that, when the snow melted, white camouflage had to be abandoned instantly had been forgotten and had to be relearned at the cost of a number of lives.

Following upon success in North Africa, plans had been made for visual display. Several Royal Engineer field companies were trained to operate deceptive devices before crossing the Channel. They were equipped with inflatable tanks, lorries and gun tractors and the kind of simulation for which they prepared ranged from tanks in harbour, to building dummy Bailey bridges with all the paraphernalia (or 'signatures' as this was technically known) and artillery dug in, accompanied by its own transport. Although the break-out from the Normandy beachhead provided opportunities for a few small-scale ruses, after reaching the Rhine the sappers reverted to their more prosaic role of road-making and other constructional work.

As indicated already sonic warfare (now known by the code name 'Poplin') was an important feature of 'Overlord' deception. In particular, motor launches operated off the French coast east of the assault area obtaining their effects from recorded battle noises in addition to smoke and radar. But the two light scout car companies accompanying the British forces did not perhaps make the impact expected, though they did go into action in Normandy and the Rhineland and earned the commendation of Montgomery.

Smoke, however, was used frequently to conceal troop concentrations, bridges and airfields, a notable object being the screening of cargo being discharged in the 'Mulberry' harbours. Special companies were formed to operate the generators in a tactical role, such operations being envisaged for deception, a screen from ground and air observation (usually artillery observation posts), to cover the clearance of obstacles such as minefields, and to protect a river crossing. Experiments had been made in using smoke while training for continental operations, but no enthusiasm had been aroused for this form of cover. Too often meteorological conditions were unfavourable and unless the troops were extremely proficient in direction finding they were prone to lose their way. For these reasons smoke was not often used in the battle area.

One notable exception was the crossing of the Rhine in March 1945, when the two British corps concentrating for this set-piece attack were covered by a smoke screen fifty miles long. Surprise was impossible to achieve, but by stopping and relighting the screen the enemy might be confused as to the timing of the operation. This also enabled aerial photographic reconnaissance of the enemy positions otherwise shrouded in smoke to take place. Shortly before the crossing, a further requirement was added to mask the artillery massed for the preparatory bombardment. The smoke penetrated to a depth of at least three miles across the Rhine and caused a good deal of discomfort among the German troops.

After the war the smoke companies were disbanded, as it was believed they could serve no useful purpose in the future.

6 WITH INTENT TO DECEIVE

It is perfectly justifiable to deceive the enemy.
                              Winston Churchill, 11 November 1942

The proving ground of the British Army in the early years of the war was the Western Desert. In the period from Wavell's victory over the Italians in the autumn of 1940 to Montgomery's defeat of Rommel two years later, British commanders were initiated into the techniques of mobile warfare. They were now able to revive the art of generalship lost in the mud of Flanders. Surprise and deception could once again be practised, making, as it was said, the desert the tactician's paradise and the quartermaster's nightmare. Camouflage, in the sense of visual deception, was practised on a scale which rivalled, and technically surpassed, Ludendorff's offensives in 1918 and Allenby's stratagems against the Turks in Palestine. The desert, which could not provide concealment, compelled the British Army to use deception. And for once it was used on a grand scale.

But camouflage to be successful had to be an integral part of the plan of operations. This could only be conceived at the highest level and there had to be mutual trust between staff officers and camouflage officers. Fortunately, there were senior staff officers prepared to treat the camoufleurs not as 'long-haired artists' in uniform but as specialists who could make an important contribution to the battle. They were lucky in the small unmilitary group of artists, architects and film producers who arrived in Cairo in the early part of 1941—men not only with artistic vision but also able to use materials with imagination.

Their leader was Geoffrey Barkas, an infantryman of World War I, who had since then made educational films. As Director of Camouflage at GHQ in Cairo he convinced the operations staff that camouflage implied much more than mere passive concealment.[1] With Barkas were three artists, John Hutton, a New Zealander who later engraved the great glass windows in Coventry Cathedral, P. E. Phillips and Blair Hughes-Stanton, painter and engraver. (Hughes-Stanton later went to Greece where he was taken prisoner and shot through the jaw by one of his captors. After many months in prison hospitals he was repatriated.) While Barkas and Hughes-Stanton took the Western Desert as their province, Hutton went to the Sudan and Phillips to Palestine, their first task being to get the lie of the land and accustom their eyes to the strongly illuminated landscape, so different from the hedgerows and coppices of England. In these lands the accent was on light, requiring natural hessian for garnishing nets and light colours for vehicles. One advantage compared to western Europe was the abundance of local materials such as canes, hurdles and matting which could be purchased in the local bazaars.

On their first trip into the desert, Barkas and Hughes-Stanton made three important discoveries: first, that despite the openness of the desert, the detritus of war—which included vehicle tracks, abandoned dumps and slit trenches—afforded ample opportunities for concealment; second, that tanks and artillery, provided they would forego their usual methods of employment, could be disguised sufficiently to satisfy the curiosity of low-flying reconnaissance aircraft; third, that the desert terrain with its escarpments and depressions was a suitable background for placing instruments of deception in the shape of dummy weapons, vehicles and installations of all kinds.

The wide perimeter of Tobruk, besieged during the summer of 1941, contained a microcosm of every variety of military activity. It was a base where supplies were discharged from shipping; aircraft operated from improvised landing grounds and the area was defended by coastal and anti-aircraft batteries from sea and air attack; and supported by their artillery the infantry patrolled the perimeter.[2]

Patch net concealing entrance to cave headquarters at Tobruk designed to blend with the surrounding rocky ground (*Public Record Office*)

By that time another twelve camouflage officers had reached the Middle East, among them were Steven Sykes and Jasper Maskelyne who, it will be recalled, were early graduates of Farnham. Maskelyne's principal duty was to provide counterfeit currency notes and other properties for agents, though his credibility on arrival in Egypt was slightly diminished when he complained of lack of cash. Other artists recently introduced to camouflage included John Codner, Robert

Medley, who proved to be a good organiser, and E. C. Calligan, who had made a mark as a commercial artist. Peter Proud, a film producer, was attached to the Australians in Tobruk when, after the main German attack had been repulsed that May, the garrison settled down to a form of siege warfare involving vigorous patrolling and small operations designed to improve local positions and to assist Wavell's ill-fated counter-offensive 'Battleaxe'.

An imaginative deception scheme was organised by Proud which, although not executed in full, provided a pointer to the way camouflage might be organised in future. It was distinguished by rapid improvisation. Ten tons of useless Italian flour made an effective adhesive with which to apply sand to vehicles and tents to make them inconspicuous. Two thousand gallons of Worcester sauce unfit for human consumption were used to thin paint. Battered petrol tins dipped in cement made dummy rocks and tubular scaffolding provided the basis for dummy artillery. Clever use was made of netting— on the one hand, to provide a false crest on the ground and so shelter a troop of artillery from enemy observation, also causing many shells to explode harmlessly behind and on either side of it; and, on the other hand, nets fixed horizontally to the superstructures of destroyers in the harbour gradually descending to the quayside successfully broke up shadows which would otherwise have given the vessels away on aerial photographs. Concealment of movement was needed in one defile. A screen 900ft long and 16ft high was erected and was kept in position by poles and pickets. It was made up of 35ft by 35ft nets garnished with hessian. Although it attracted the attention of dive-bombers, because of its floppy, resilient weave, only slight damage was caused. Two of the enemy were shot down in the attack.

A building of considerable importance was the distillery which purified drinking water for the garrison. The impression was to be given that it had been badly damaged in an air raid so that it would be removed from the enemy's target list. Proud darkened certain areas on the building to suggest bomb damage and the plant functioned throughout the siege. Vehicles too dark in colour had to be given lighter coats of paint. This operation was effectively combined with a deception operation, the purpose of which was to create a scene of great activity. Near the desired spot Proud placed a 'Camouflage Service Station', plainly advertised. Passing truck drivers were drawn by notices inviting them to 'camouflage while you wait' which in no time attracted a long queue of vehicles taking advantage of a job, for once, done by someone else.

From these slightly bizarre efforts carried out with the help of a section of Royal Australian Engineers and a company of Indian pioneers several important lessons were learned. Firstly, camouflage was too complex to be left entirely to amateurs. Officers and men

Obvious road junction at Rond Point, an aiming point for the water works at Alexandria. Head covers have been erected to conform with patterns of buildings
(*Public Record Office*)

would have to be trained in the technical aspects and senior officers would have to understand what was meant by terms such as disruption, background and behaviour, countershading, the interpretation of air photographs and deception. Second, workshops were required to produce materials in large quantities. In one year alone, for example, 8,000 tons of paint were consumed in camouflage and 120 million yards of hessian were used to garnish nets.

In response to the first requirement a camouflage training and development centre was set up at Helwan in the desert near Cairo. In charge was a regular soldier, Maj J. Sholto Douglas of the Royal Scots.[3] Hugh Cott was the chief instructor who in his spare moments could be found attending to the snakes, beetles and lizards which he kept in petrol cans. From time to time he would disappear into the forward area to supervise camouflage schemes. A number of young officers from a variety of units were trained here and provided a valuable reserve for the handful of professional camoufleurs referred to in the following pages. The centre also indoctrinated large numbers

of soldiers in the elementary principles of camouflage, such as understanding the nature of colour in the desert, and posters and pamphlets
(one lively one written by Barkas himself) were produced to keep these
principles fresh in their minds.

The second requirement was met by the formation of No 85 (South
African) Camouflage Company under Maj Derek Van Berg, a
Johannesburg architect, assisted by Anthony Ayrton, son of the well-
known architect, Maxwell Ayrton, and who later died from illness
in Tunisia. This unit comprised a workshops and six mobile detachments. Next to take the field was No 1 Camouflage Company RE,
composed of British and Palestinian Jews who had volunteered to
serve in the British Army; it was commanded by a Rhodesian, Maj
V. W. Hampson.

In 'Crusader', the attempt by Auchinleck to destroy Rommel's
armoured forces, isolate his troops on the Egyptian frontier, and link
up with the beleaguered garrison in Tobruk, camouflage was planned
not only for protection but to coincide with the strategic and tactical
plan.[4] This elevation of camouflage was mainly because of the good
impression made by Barkas on the Director of Military Operations,
Brig J. F. M. (later Sir John) Whiteley. The actual responsibility for
execution of the plans lay in the capable hands of Steven Sykes, who
had been trained as a sapper, and who appreciated how much camouflage could influence the battle. Other camouflage officers attached
to the 8th Army were the sculptor Bainbridge Copnall and the
painters Robert Medley and John Codner.

Strategically, the intention was to distract the attention of the
enemy from the north coast by suggesting concentrations to the south
at the oasis of Siwa and at Giarabut. Dummy vehicles were brought
into the area and camouflaged and dummy latrines, cook houses and
anti-aircraft gun positions constructed. The whole operation would
last about a fortnight and fit in with troop movements, both real and
false in the general cover plan.

Unfortunately resources were inadequate and the deception went
off at half cock. There were insufficient vehicles to give the impression
of 'busy' tracks leading to the concentration area. Traffic diversions
outside camp areas to simulate the movement of large forces did not
always take place; there were too few vehicles to carry camouflage
materials into the forward area; and the timing of troop and vehicle
movements was not worked out in sufficient detail. Although German
intelligence did overestimate the actual strength in the deception area,
Barkas doubted whether camouflage could take much of the credit—
it was the result more of false moves by motor transport.

The tactical deception plan was to induce the enemy to believe
that a feint attack was to be made on Bardia on the coast east of
Tobruk. Dummy tanks were placed in hull-down positions, with a

Dummy rail head designed to divert enemy bombers from the real one at Capuzzo on the Egyptian frontier (*Public Record Office*)

few real armoured vehicles moving round them to give an air of authenticity and columns of lorries created clouds of dust. But the scale of deception was too small to be really convincing.

One sensitive target over which great care had to be taken was the rail terminal at Capuzzo that, according to Barkas, 'screamed its existence and its purpose into the sky'. As it was the main line of communication for the desert army, the enemy made strenuous attempts to destroy it, including an abortive raid by one of the daring Italian naval assault teams which landed from motor boats. But their cache of explosives was detonated by a British soldier on patrol who unwittingly threw a cigarette end on to it. It was therefore decided to construct a dummy railhead south of the real terminal. Largely Sykes's creation, the line was made out of beaten-out 4-gallon petrol tins. It was just under seven miles long and the constructors adhered to a strict timetable so that the enemy would not become suspicious. The rolling-stock was made of canvas fixed to poles. As the exact height of the wagons could not be attained, the gauge of the dummy track was gradually reduced on the last lap. Local materials such as palm-frond hurdles—normally issued to make box beds—salvaged hessian and scrap served to make ramps, sidings and water tanks. A dummy locomotive, complete with soya stove and chimney belching smoke, box wagons and flat cars were provided. Aircraft duly attacked the dummy terminal on the first night after completion, and in the excitement of the moment Sykes detonated eleven decoy fires which did not quite coincide with the number of bombs dropped. However, about half the number of bombs destined for Capuzzo fell in the open desert.

The ebb and flow of the fighting marked by Rommel's spring offensive of 1942 and the withdrawal of the British and Common-

Improvised Crusader tank displayed in connection with dummy rail head scheme
(*Public Record Office*)

wealth troops to El Alamein were not conducive to camouflage schemes. A number of these were planned and begun, only to be abandoned in the fluid battle. Similarly the return of the Afrika Korps put an end to the development of a mock harbour between Benghazi and Derna. The idea was to continue the work begun by the Italians and included the boring of a tunnel through a shoulder of rock. A canvas drop sheet indicated that the tunnel was being continued and dummy construction camps, stores and vehicles were erected in the vicinity. Barkas pointed out that the unmasking of one scheme did not mean that the camoufleurs were wasting their time. Provided that the enemy's intelligence was efficient and reacted to what the camera or the eye revealed he was for ever capable of being deceived.

Concealment and deception, to be of any value, required time. This was provided after Auchinleck, a firm believer in this form of warfare, had finally checked the German and Italian advance on the Egyptian frontier in July 1942, and after his successor, Montgomery, had decisively frustrated Rommel's desperate attempt to break through the British defences at Alam Halfa that September. There was now a period of seven weeks before the launching of Montgomery's offensive at El Alamein on the night of 23 October. The camouflage organisation thus had the time to prepare materials and to lay out schemes. Another important factor was that the Royal Air Force's superiority in the air made enemy air reconnaissance much more difficult and it was largely restricted to high-level photographic flights.

Montgomery's final plan was to make the main thrust in the north with the infantry divisions of 30th Corps punching a hole through which the armoured divisions of 10th Corps would pour to cut the enemy's supply routes, while a diversionary attack by 13th Corps

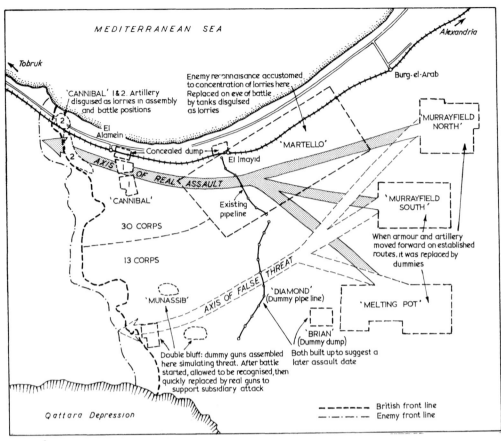

MEDITERRANEAN SEA

Alexandria

Tobruk

'CANNIBAL' 1&2. Artillery
disguised as lorries in assembly
and battle positions

Enemy reconnaisance accustomed
to concentration of lorries here.
Replaced on eve of battle
by tanks disguised
as lorries

Burg·el·Arab

El
Alamein

Concealed dump

'MARTELLO'

El Imayid

'MURRAYFIELD
NORTH'

AXIS OF REAL ASSAULT

'CANNIBAL'

Existing
pipeline

'MURRAYFIELD
SOUTH'

30 CORPS

When armour and artillery
moved forward on established
routes, it was replaced by
dummies

13 CORPS

AXIS OF FALSE THREAT

'MUNASSIB'

'DIAMOND'
(Dummy pipe line)

'MELTING POT'

'BRIAN'
(Dummy dump)

Both built up to suggest a
later assault date

Double bluff: dummy guns assembled
here simulating threat. After battle
started, allowed to be recognised, then
quickly replaced by real guns to
support subsidiary attack

Qattara Depression

------- British front line
·—·—·—· Enemy front line

Deception plan for the battle of El Alamein, 23 October 1942
(*Imperial War Museum*)

would distract the enemy's attention in the south. Barkas and his
fellow camoufleurs had, first, to conceal as far as possible the true
nature of the preparations in the north and where concealment was
impossible to minimise their significance. Second, they had to make
the enemy believe that the battle would begin two or three days later
than might be anticipated by slowing down the apparent rate of
build-up. Third, they had to suggest that a substantial attack would
be mounted in the south.

All the resources of camouflage were pressed into operations
involving quantities of labour, transport and the mass production of
deception devices.[5] The task of concealment and display was undertaken by Ayrton and Brian Robb, well known as an illustrator, who
since then has achieved distinction as a painter. Barkas and Maj R. J.
Southron, a capable tank corps officer, supervised the provision of
materials and the manufacture of devices. Southron succeeded Barkas
as Director of Camouflage when the latter took up an appointment
with the Directorate of Special Weapons and Vehicles in London.

An essential element of the concealment scheme in the north was
to lead the enemy to believe that, while vehicles were assembling here,

the armour was heading south. To this end 10th Corps was to advance in a series of stages, the final launching-pad for the assault being known as 'Martello', into which the tanks would move just before D-day. Places were prepared for the armour and in the interim were occupied by lorries. On the appropriate night these vehicles were to be surreptitiously replaced by tanks. The enemy would, it was anticipated, be unaware that the lorries had gone by the draping of canvas covers known as 'Sunshades' over the tanks, making them resemble soft-skinned vehicles. This ruse sprang several years earlier from Wavell's brain and he had sketched a design from which a prototype might be made. Over a thousand were produced.

The infantry assault was to be preceded by a massive bombardment and here again it was necessary to conceal the massing of artillery. The 25-pounders towed by their conspicuous tractors, known as 'quads', were made under the supervision of Sydney Robinson, seconded from the Royal Armoured Corps, to resemble 3-ton lorries by a canopy of nets and poles known as a 'Cannibal'.

As important as the disguise of weapons and vehicles was the concealment of some 6,000 tons of supplies of various kinds. Several ingenious ideas were proposed by Ayrton and put into effect by Robinson. Slit trenches were dug ostensibly for use as fire positions, but the walls were reinforced by 'masonry' in the form of petrol tins, the presence of which were not betrayed by excrescence of shadow. Food supplies were stacked in the shape of 3-ton lorries and covered with camouflage nets, the whole area giving the appearance of dispersed vehicles.

All these schemes were, it must be emphasised, designed to encourage German intelligence to believe that the 8th Army's concentration was indeed reaching its peak but some time before the real D-day, and that the indications were that the armour was heading southwards. Substance was given to this development by the construction of a dummy pipeline. Supervised by Philip Cornish, the idea was to extend a real pipeline to the south-west. A trench was dug in the normal way in stretches of five miles at a time. The dummy pipes were made out of 4-gallon non-returnable petrol tins and were laid alongside the trench. At night they were moved forward to the next stretch and the trench filled in. The pipeline's appearance was further enhanced by dummy pump houses, overhead tanks and can-filling stations. At certain points dummy vehicles and men were dispersed in the vicinity.

The strength of the diversion was further reinforced by the creation of a large depot. Camouflaged stores were erected over a wide area and gave the illusion of dispersed oil, petrol and ammunition dumps. These preparations began about a fortnight before D-day and although disturbed by tanks passing through the area (their tracks

'Sunshade' canvas cover erected on tank to make it look like a lorry
(*Public Record Office*)

'Cannibal' Gun and limber disguised to look like a truck
(*Public Record Office*)

had to be eliminated) and by sand storms, the work was completed with two days to spare.

Meanwhile, to the north, the difficult task of deceiving the Germans over the actual start of the assault was in progress. Along the Munassib Ridge measures were taken to make the enemy believe that a number of guns were dummies by not maintaining the camouflage. On the eve of the attack the dummies were replaced by real guns and their crews. At the same time in another sector dummy figures were to be manipulated by the 9th Australian Division in a 'Chinese Attack', a revival of a form of diversion used, as has been seen, in World War I.

More difficult was the movement forward of 10th Corps armour before D-day. The initial advance forward took place conspicuously so that the German tactical reconnaissance aircraft could make the required deduction—that of moves to the south-west. But the utmost security had to be taken over the final move into 'Martello'. The provision of hiding places there has already been explained. Now it was necessary to show that the intermediate transit area had not been vacated. At the last moment the camouflage development centre at Helwan went into action and, employing three pioneer companies, assisted by local labour, created dummies for 500 guns and 2,000 vehicles. Under the direction of John Baker, the pioneers cut and bound brushwood hurdles into suitable shapes, cut and stitched patches of hessian to the wooden frameworks and, finally, painted and embellished them with detail. Welcome assistance was provided at the last moment by No 1 Camouflage Company.

The clandestine move of the tanks into 'Martello' was accomplished according to plan by first light on 21 October. As each unit moved out, camouflage parties put up replicas of guns and vehicles. This transposition, together with the erasure of tracks as far as possible, was completed on the eve of D-day.

The opening assault failed, in the event, to break through the German positions, nor did the 13th Corps' feint in the south achieve its intention of distracting the German armour. Nevertheless the preponderance of British tanks, covered by the ubiquitous Royal Air Force, enabled them to win the day just over a week later. The miscarriage of the first attempt had little to do with the effectiveness of the concealment and deception plans, without which there might have been much greater frustration of the 8th Army's hopes to eliminate once and for all the threat to Cairo and the Suez Canal.

During the ensuing advance of the 8th Army on Tunisia, several small deception operations were arranged by 30th Corps, to which Sydney Robinson was attached as camouflage officer. At that time Gen Anderson's 1st Army was battling with the enemy in Tunisia alongside the Americans, opposing the Germans and the Italians for the first time. Indeed, for most of the troops, whether British or

Dummy 25 pounder gun in British 30th Corps area improvised from local materials (*Public Record Office*)

American, it was their first taste of action. Capt Godfrey Baxter, an officer of great resource and courage and in peacetime a West End theatrical producer, landed with 1st Army Headquarters as its camouflage officer and was later assisted by two lieutenants, Allen and Hamilton, the latter an architect. Starting literally from nothing, they scrounged hessian from army stores and other materials such as charcoal bags and rush prayer mats from the local bazaars and in a short while had organised three small sections for 5th and 9th Corps and Army HQ. Baxter was later killed, after he had attached himself unofficially to a commando group. Officers from the American camouflage battalion liaised closely with their British counterparts.

Although on a less ambitious scale than El Alamein, a number of the deceptions received commendation from Gen Alexander, the commander-in-chief. Two in particular are worth noting. One occurred when the 1st Armoured Division was transferred from the 8th Army to the 1st Army and the camouflage section was given two days in which to repaint vehicles, arrange a false display and provide concealment. The second was during the final drive against the Germans when seventy dummy tanks were assembled as a feint to induce the enemy to believe that Gen Anderson had split his armoured forces.

Throughout this period the bases and rear areas with their vital depots had to be protected against air attack. Dummy aircraft and decoy fires similar to those in England were created, often with effect. Attention to detail was, of course, always necessary as when, on one occasion, some dummy aircraft were destroyed during a raid on an airfield but the wreckage was not removed as was normally the custom. The following night another raid was experienced, the decoy operators congratulating themselves on their success though somewhat perplexed by the lack of explosions. Daylight revealed a number of craters containing dummy bombs.

Harbour facilities at the ports of Oran, Algiers, Bougie, Bizerta, Sousse and Sfax now assumed great importance, for from them were soon to be mounted the amphibious assaults against Sicily and southern Italy. Smoke-screens now came into their own.[7] They were ignited by special pioneer companies trained in the operation of the British No 24 Generator and the American M1 smoke pot, usually known as an Esso. Whereas the British model generated black smoke, the American smoke was whiter in colour and more effective in a daylight raid. These generators were also easy to transport and for this reason the British smoke companies were, as far as possible, equipped with M1s. Smoke-screens were required to be operated as soon as a port had been taken over by the ground troops and the vital area was usually being obscured within twenty-four hours. Their effectiveness depended on receiving warning of attack through the radar screen, and their density was always dependent on the direction of the wind.

Smoke was also used in the battle area.[8] At Salerno ships discharging supplies off the beaches were screened by smoke, though it proved to be a hindrance rather than a help. In the beachhead the infantry were equipped with smoke pots to cover their flanks from observed artillery fire. Smoke was used in support of river crossings, for example, at the crossing of the Garigliano.

Accompanying the 8th Army in their advance through Italy were No 1 Camouflage Company, now wholly Palestinian and commanded by Maj L. Aronov,[9] No 85 (South African) Camouflage Company, and B Camouflage Section RE (about thirty-five all ranks) under Capt N. A. Critchley of 5th Corps, which had been formed in Tunisia to experiment with deception devices and to advise non-specialists on how to make and use camouflage and deception material. They received their instructions through Robb and Cornish, who were in touch with the planning staff at Headquarters, 8th Army. Although the workshop sections of these companies continued to make devices, the supply situation had so improved that they were receiving from England dummy Shermans and Churchills, either inflatable or capable of being dismantled quickly, dummy trucks, lorries and various types of artillery.

New problems faced the camoufleurs. The armies were operating in hilly, often rugged, country, pierced by numerous rivers providing ideal lines of defence for the enemy. The ground was punctuated by farms, fields, vineyards and olive groves affording good cover and making unnecessary the wide dispersion of vehicles. Correspondingly, the opportunities for deploying large numbers of dummy vehicles as in the desert no longer existed. The countryside was, moreover, inhabited by a peasantry usually friendly but inveterate gossips, and this could either help or endanger concealment or deception schemes. Although the Allies had, by and large, mastery of the air, there was always the possibility of a high-level photo-reconnaissance plane obtaining valuable information.

German 105mm gun at Enfidaville, Tunisia camouflaged by brushwood. Note absence of pit and very few tracks on ground which would make it conspicuous
(*Public Record Office*)

At the same time the Italian peninsula was ideal for deception operations. On both sides were beaches suggesting possible landing places and the roads, however rudimentary, enabled formations to be switched from one side to the other with comparative ease.

Rome and the country beyond were the Allied objectives in early 1944, but the Germans were strongly ensconced in natural defensive lines to which they had given code names such as 'Gustav' or 'Hitler' and which contained as a pivot that seemingly impregnable fortress, the monastery of Monte Cassino. The Germans had also contained the Allied landings at Anzio. An all-out effort was planned for May, which involved moving the bulk of the 8th Army westward from the Adriatic. This was to be accompanied by elaborate camouflage and deception.[11] The deception plan was to induce the enemy to believe that another amphibious attack was to be made at Civitavecchia north of Rome and make him hesitate to commit his reserves south of Rome. In order to simulate preparations for this operation, dummy landing craft, rafts, hards and gantries were erected by the British camouflage experts on the east coast at Termoli and Barletta, much of the work taking place in high winds and rain. In the Naples–Salerno area the impression of amphibious training was given by a few ships and dummy wireless traffic and Canadian Corps signs were set up on the roads. Additional realism was provided by air reconnaissances and attacks on coastal targets along the coast north of Rome.

Meanwhile the concentration for the real attack in the Liri Valley had to be carefully concealed. Wireless traffic was controlled to give the impression that some three divisions had been withdrawn for amphibious training. Every care was taken to conceal troop movements opposite the enemy. Much of this work was non-specialist and could be done by the troops themselves under direction of their unit camouflage officers. They erected vertical screens to prevent observation from the monastery of Cassino and concealed their guns and other equipment with nets and foliage. But there were other items which required the skilled attention of the camouflage companies— supply dumps, bridging equipment and self-propelled guns. These experts also painted tentage, designed sniper's suits and collapsible bushes behind which a marksman could fire, brought forward on mountain tracks and erected dummy tanks, and operated flash simulators made of black powder and cordite for the gunners, though in time the latter took on this job themselves, synchronising dummy with real bombardments.

At the time it was believed that the deception scheme had influenced the German command to expect another seaborne assault and the camoufleurs had been congratulated on their work at Termoli by Maj-Gen G. P. Walsh, the chief of staff, 8th Army and an old desert hand. It is likely, however, that the German commander-in-chief, Kesselring, was convinced that the Allies would take advantage of their superior naval power and the deception was perhaps less effective than was thought.

The camouflage of the German Army, though not much in evidence in the desert, proved to be extremely adaptable in the close fighting in which they were now engaged. Though by British and American standards less well-equipped with artificial materials, such as nets, their basic camouflage training now came into its own and they put local materials to good use, especially in the Gustav Line and other positions. The reversible sniper's tunics worn by the paratroops, who so often formed the backbone of the stubborn rearguard actions, green on one side and brown on the other (possibly copied from the Russian snipers), blended into the background, though the outline was often identifiable. Their siting of positions, as always the

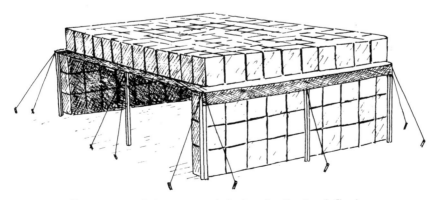

Dummy petrol depot erected during the Battle of Cassino
(*Public Record Office*)

key to good concealment, was difficult to fault. As Allied mastery of the air increased, so German camouflage improved; dummy bridges were made of baulks of timber, dummy trenches (*schein stellungen*) and guns simulated by tree trunks and a suitable disposition of farm carts were all brought into play.[12]

Dummy supply depot (Detail Issue Depot) characteristic of deception schemes in the Italian campaign, 1944 (*Public Record Office*)

The hard fighting south of Rome culminated in the link-up with the Anzio beachhead and the advance on Rome, which was entered on 4 June. In a few weeks the Allied armies, now reduced in size because of demands from the battle in France, faced the Gothic Line, extending roughly between Pisa and Rimini. It had been intended that the main thrust should be in the centre, matched by a simulated strike up the Adriatic coast by the British, the Americans aiming at Genoa.[13] A good deal of work had already been done, including the building of a dummy supply depot and headquarters for 5th Corps, during which straw was scattered over the area to give the impression that the ground was being constantly traversed.

Early in August the new 8th Army commander, Oliver Leese, decided to reverse the plan and make the main thrust towards Rimini, followed by an American attack on Bologna. Although surprise was achieved, operations were eventually bogged down by stubborn enemy resistance and by bad weather. Much of the dummy material laid for the original scheme was left to rot on the ground.

But in the final battle of the 8th Army the following spring, designed to trap the German forces south of the river Po, the camoufleurs' work was not wasted.[14] The British were to break through the so-called Argenta 'gap', to the west of Lake Commachio, leading into the plain beyond. The impression that there would be a landing north of the Po was to be strengthened by the capture of the spit of land separating Commachio from the sea. On the left of the British, the Americans were to take Bologna, still held by the enemy.

An interesting feature of the operation was the use of amphibious armoured troop-carriers, known as Fantails, which were to make a flanking attack over the lake and surrounding countryside flooded by the Germans. It was essential that the enemy should not know of the presence of these vehicles in Italy, as there were several hundred of them—and special arrangements were made to conceal them during the training period on Lake Trasimene and for their assembly on the shores of Lake Commachio. B Section built special hangars for the training period and in the forward area constructed hides in the woods around Ravenna, the vehicles being driven under nets suspended from trees. Tracks had to be eliminated after their move into the forward area. Surprise was achieved, although aerial photographs taken by the Germans did reveal a Fantail but it was by then too late to take action against them.

Philip Cornish managed the deception plan in the Commachio Spit. All the usual properties were used, such as dummy bridging dumps, artillery, simulated gunfire and smoke-screens. Dummy landing craft on the coast indicated that a major landing would take place. Commandos and a brigade of Guards operated in conjunction with the dummy preparations, diverting the enemy while the main British attack went through the 'gap'. Within three weeks the German forces in Italy had surrendered.

In the Burmese jungle, as opposed to the desert, visibility was greatly reduced, especially in the Arakan where razor-backed ridges are covered with dense mixed forest including bamboo. In these regions opportunities for display were limited, but sonic warfare could be practised on a large scale, always remembering that it had to be carried out against a background noise of birds, monkeys, crickets and other denizens of the undergrowth. Much of the country is hilly and this made concealment from Japanese observation posts of paramount importance. At the same time there was little to worry from the Japanese Air Force, whose reconnaissances were few and far between. In camouflaging defensive positions, the jungle had to be left unharmed and track discipline could not be neglected because after rain, paths or tracks made across hill crests showed up clearly.

The Japanese infantry were expert in siting their bunkers on the tops of hill features or on reverse slopes. They were built of thick logs and were so well camouflaged with grass and moss, occasionally making use of nets, that they were rarely visible at ranges beyond 50yd without prolonged searching. The Japanese also made a point of using certain simple forms of deception in close jungle such as shouting false orders in English or Urdu or endeavouring to induce troops to surrender. The bodies of dead or wounded soldiers were sometimes used as decoys and attempts to recover them were countered by machine-gun fire. Dummy figures and weapons were set up on hill positions, both to draw fire and to give a false impression of strength. Above all, they favoured the use of noise to deceive and intimidate. Among such ruses were the sound of explosions coming from the rear and flanks to make their enemy think he had been surrounded; and by night they threw Chinese crackers into positions and rattled their rifle bolts.

Japanese intelligence, on the other hand, was woefully deficient and senior officers often suffered from conceit and self-deception. They invaded India through Manipur with virtually no administrative support against odds of what they believed to be about 20 to 1. Their plans were usually so inflexible that inducement by Allied deception to change them, for the most part, had no effect.

One of Wavell's first acts after becoming commander-in-chief in India in July 1941 was to set up a deception staff. India's pitifully inadequate defence forces, faced by the threat of attack from the north-west by the Germans, then advancing on Moscow, and the possibility of attack from the east by Japan (Pearl Harbor was only six months away) would have to resort to bluff where equipment did not exist.

André Bicât, painter and sculptor, accompanied by a handful of artists, designers and architects, which included the architect Michael, brother of Philip, Powell, soon to be celebrated by his partnership with John Moya in British post-war building, and the painter Philip Suffolk, had arrived in Kirkee, near Poona, shortly after the fall of Singapore to instruct the Indian Army in the art of camouflage.[15] Current doctrine was based on static camouflage which, to Bicât, seemed irrelevant to the requirements of the war in the jungle, and after overcoming initial opposition, formed at GHQ New Delhi a camouflage development section under the Director of Military Intelligence, Brig W. J. Cawthorn, who was enthusiastic about its potentialities. (Bicât's assurance that he could manufacture 500 dummy tanks when only five real ones were available to defend India was a convincing argument that camouflage was worthwhile.)

In time this small unit, which began life in an office of the bandsmen's quarters on the Viceroy's estate, became the Inter-Service Technical Bureau under Bicât, then a lieutenant-colonel, a large organisation embracing several factories or depots near the front which produced simulators for rifle fire, smoke generators—including one made out of bamboo—a special mortar bomb containing battle noises, all kinds of dummies from mock-up landing craft to folding trucks and Stuart tanks, from gliders to men, mules and elephants.[16] It owed its success to the enthusiasm of its members, who indefatigably sought suitable local materials such as basketwork for dummy aircraft, and their experiments with pyrotechnic devices and bombs containing propaganda leaflets were often hazardous, but fortunately never fatal. Most of these devices were approved after demonstrations attended by senior officers who could relax from their paper work for an hour or so.

Less romantic, though just as essential, was the requirement for face cream to be applied to British officers and other ranks on jungle patrols.[17] If officers were made to look too like the men they commanded, the possibility of confusion arose, and the actions demanded of an officer were self-indicative, but it was found that face-darkening helped, particularly where British officers commanded Indian units and became obvious targets for snipers. The cream was sent out from England and was a compound of vanishing cream, yellow ochre, carbon black and vaseline and was intended to be proof against rain and sweat. Local plant juices, supposed to have beneficial qualities, according to Ayurvedic doctors, were not used as it was found that they had 'a very astringent nature and [were] unpleasant when applied to the delicate skin surrounding the eyes, etc'.

But the section's most interesting work was for the small units engaged in deception, subversion and other forms of clandestine warfare such as the Secret Intelligence Service, the Political Warfare Executive and SOE. A printing press was acquired from the Congress Party, whose leaders were then in gaol, to make currency notes for agents and a special process for staining the notes to make them appear used supplanted laborious rubbing by the hands of female workers.

A frequent customer for Bicât's properties was Peter Fleming, the celebrated writer, who had recently travelled extensively in Central Asia and had been involved in deception since Dunkirk. At that time a lieutenant-colonel, he was in charge of D Division whose role was to persuade the Japanese that the British, American and Chinese forces were generally superior in strength and located in positions thinly held by real units. D Division employed a variety of methods, mainly by the wireless transmission of dummy orders of battle and indiscreetly revealing through conversations between staff officers future movements of formations. But there were a number of occasions when visual display was used. One of the first was modelled on the haversack stained with fresh blood, containing papers, letters and money, dropped during Allenby's advance on Jerusalem and which deceived the Turks into preparing for an attack from another direction. During the retreat from Rangoon Wavell's car was deliberately wrecked on the far side of the Ava bridge, from which the British had just withdrawn, and his kit and a number of secret documents left inside it.

Another ruse involved a sketch book containing drawings of officers and other ranks, disclosing their formation signs and locations (prepared by Suffolk), which appeared to have been carelessly dropped by a war artist. It was intended to provoke the Japanese intelligence staff into revising their British order of battle. False information was also fed by the dropping by air of a corpse, complete with unopened parachute and carrying a portable radio transmitter, over Japanese-occupied territory. The Japanese were expected to use the set to counter D Division's activities and in so doing disclose more than they were able to discover. But this scheme proved to be too sophisticated and Fleming's assistants concluded that the effort they had put into body-snatching in Calcutta in the height of the hot weather and in the middle of a famine hardly compensated for the negative result. In the longer term, strategic plans associated with amphibious operations along the coast towards Rangoon were constantly having to be abandoned due to the shortage of landing craft and so upsetting the carefully designed deception schemes. However, when Fleming at the end of the war reviewed the activities of D Division, while acknowledging that their successes were limited by the self-deception and ignorance of Japanese intelligence, he asked what would have happened 'had they accurately appreciated our strength and real intentions'.

A better reaction seems to have been obtained through tactical deception carried out by D Force under Lt-Col P. E. X. Turnbull, but which did not start operating until October 1944 when the British and Indian forces under Slim had begun the return march to Rangoon. These operations were short term and limited to the battle area. Turnbull's headquarters at Calcutta directed three units. The first was concerned with the deployment of static and mobile dummies (usually tanks) and was given the title of No 303 Indian Brigade; it had been transferred to India from Persia for this purpose.[18] Organised into six observation squadrons, each under two British officers and thirty British and Indian other ranks, it began to operate under the orders of Cawthorn towards the end of 1943. Two squadrons saw action in the Arakan, Manipur, and accompanied Wingate's airborne incursion behind the Japanese lines. They were trained to erect road screens, dummy tanks and vehicles made out of scrim, supported by bamboos cut in the jungle; and they were accomplished in the use of pyrotechnic devices, including one variety known as 'Bicât's sausages'.

Eventually No 303 Brigade amalgamated with Nos 4 and 5 Light Scout Car Companies under Maj Llewellyn which, it will be recalled, had been demanded by Wavell, to provide greater mobility. Each unit, numbering no more than thirty-four all ranks, took part in actions along the entire front, most of the time in close proximity to the enemy. Though car crews were chosen for their technical ability, they also had to use their arms in an emergency, and in so doing one of their officers, Lt C. E. Raymond, won the Victoria Cross.

While visual display and battle noises were D Force's stock in trade, it also transmitted records of Japanese speech through loudspeakers. But difficulties were often experienced in getting the equipment forward in a jeep. On the whole less sophisticated methods seem to have been more valuable such as spreading rumours among local villages, lighting fires and cutting wood in areas known to be under observation by the Japanese, and the dropping of blood-soaked bandages on tracks, to give the appearance of a withdrawing patrol.

D Force also executed a number of small dummy airborne operations with varying degrees of success. Dummy paratroops were dropped, Very light signals fired and pyrotechnic devices simulated rifle fire and the throwing of grenades. The advantage of such operations was that only a very small effort was required to produce quite extensive results. Equipment carried in one bomber aircraft could, for example, simulate a battle on the scale of a platoon lasting up to six hours.[19]

Complementing the land and airborne deception activities, a naval scout unit was formed early in 1945 to operate in the Akyab area north of Rangoon in support of the various amphibious operations that were planned but rarely executed because of lack of resources. It was in one of these inlets lined by mud banks that one of the best English water-colour painters, Vivian Pitchforth, then attached to a Royal Marine Commando unit as a war artist, was asked by the commanding officer to supervise the painting of some assault craft. So effectively did they merge into their surroundings when moored that several were actually missing for some time.

The tour de force of deception operations against the Japanese, known as 'Cloak', during the final advance into Burma was in aid of the crossing of the river Irrawaddy—a major obstacle—in February 1945. Slim's intention was to conceal the crossing until the last possible moment by persuading the Japanese to believe that the force preparing to cross the river—4th Corps—was merely making a feint to distract attention from the attack on Mandalay by 33rd Corps from the north.[20] A dummy 4th Corps headquarters was substituted for the real one when it left for the Irrawaddy. Wireless signals continued to be exchanged with 33rd Corps, the real headquarters maintaining wireless silence until the last moment, and even then one of its divisional headquarters was simulated. Deliberate 'plants' by wireless were made and news broadcasts made slightly inaccurate references to units engaged. Parallel to misleading the enemy through wireless communications, there was a large dummy airborne drop, making full use of pyrotechnic devices. Although the signal deception plan was a source of irritation to the operational staffs and its enforcement tested their patience and discipline, the enemy, as Slim later wrote, was 'completely deceived into thinking that this was a diversion' to the main attack on Mandalay. There is no doubt that the speed with which the advance into central Burma was accomplished was due in no small measure to this deception scheme.

On a much less spectacular scale, a sea and airborne simulated attack against Moulmein, north of Rangoon, may have accelerated the Japanese withdrawal from the capital of Burma.

As for the American forces fighting in the south and south-west Pacific, they hardly ever used camouflage because of the failure of the Japanese to make any systematic air reconnaissance.[21] By mid-1944 overwhelming Allied air superiority made camouflage superfluous, even in most of the forward areas.

7 CONCEALING THE UNCONCEALABLE

Bad camouflage is so much labour lost and often is difficult to judge by direct experiment.

Solomon J. Solomon, RA

Camouflage can be best employed when the subject is motionless and must be discarded to some extent when active aggression or flight is commenced.

Bomber Command Staff Officer, 1944

Before the outbreak of war, ships of the Royal Navy were painted according to the station from which they were operating. In home waters the colour was dark grey; in the Mediterranean light grey; and in the Indian Ocean and Far East various tones of white were used. The criterion for paintwork was comfort for the crew rather than concealment for war.

The dazzle-painting of World War I with its strident colours of blue, black and yellow, the purpose of which was to confuse the aim of an enemy submarine, had never found much favour and in 1936 an Admiralty committee had reaffirmed this view. In the meantime, however, sea warfare had been revolutionised by shore-based as well as carrier-borne aircraft, and it seems strange that it was not until March 1940 that Adm T. S. V. (later Sir Tom) Phillips, then deputy chief of naval staff and himself to become a victim of air attack in less than a year's time when the *Repulse* and *Prince of Wales* were sunk by Japanese bombers off Malaya, admitted that the air was indeed a new problem, but did not press for any investigation on camouflage.[1]

In the US Navy, which like the British had abandoned camouflage in 1918, a rather more enlightened attitude may be traced from 1935, when the Naval Research Laboratory renewed its interest in camouflage and began to experiment with both concealment and confusion systems. A destroyer squadron carried out trials at San Diego, which resulted in a number of schemes being put into practice. As the US Navy was actively engaged in escorting convoys operating during the early period of the Lend-Lease scheme on the American side of the Atlantic, it had the opportunity to test a variety of colours and about ten schemes called 'Measures' were actually being used or were under trial before American ships were actively engaged in the battle of the Atlantic.

But in the Royal Navy camouflage was out of fashion and in the early summer of 1940 the Canadian scientist, C. F. (later Sir Charles) Goodeve, in charge of a group of scientists and engineers in naval uniform called the Directorate of Miscellaneous Weapons Development (DMWD) and responsible, among other things, for devising means for countering enemy air attack, was amazed to be told by an Admiralty colleague that not only was it official policy that there should be no camouflage, but that there should be no experiments either. Goodeve ignored this advice and instructed Donald Currie, an ex-Royal Navy officer, yachtsman and water-colour painter from Devon, to go ahead with finding out how to make merchant ships less visible, especially from the air. To the colleague, he said tersely : 'Our report will go to the First Sea Lord. If you wish I will send you a copy !'[2]

Currie's report, based on observations from ships and aircraft of merchant ships in convoy, laid down three shades of grey according to the conditions of light prevailing in the sea routes on which they were employed. They were a dark tone with a reflection factor (according to the Admiralty, the ratio of the total light flux leaving a surface by reflection to that incident on the surface) of 10 per cent which was, in fact, the colour of grey already in use on ships of the Home Fleet; a middle tone recently introduced which acquired the identification MS15 (Merchant Ships 15 per cent reflection factor); and a light grey with a reflection factor of about 30 per cent. This was the grey in use on ships of the Mediterranean Fleet. These three colours became standard and were eventually embodied in a wider range by the Admiralty.

Meanwhile captains engaged in operations against the enemy had on their own initiative begun to camouflage their charges. As the only example to hand was the so-called dazzle-painting based on 1914-18, the aim at this stage of the war was not so much to reduce visibility as to try to confuse an observer as to the ship's type and identity and her inclination—direction of movement in relation to the ship's position. As far as success was possible with this double aim it could only be achieved at the expense of a general reduction of the ship's visibility, because either the light or the dark tones which had to be used in contrast to create confusion were bound to show up unnecessarily strongly in any condition of light.

The first ships to be so painted were two destroyers, *Grenville* and *Grenade*, early in 1940 on the instructions of the commander-in-chief Western Approaches, Adm Sir Martin Dunbar-Nasmith vc, an outstanding submarine commander in World War I. *Grenville* was painted dark and light grey in irregular rhomboids and *Grenade*, later sunk off Dunkirk, was painted in dark and light grey and stone, the areas being much more irregular in shape. Shadows and the edges of vertical surfaces such as funnels, the bridge and masts, were broken up. Observations made during the Narvik operation indicated that *Grenade* had been less easy to spot than other ships. Later Capt W. (later Sir William) Tennant, commanding *Repulse*, who had experienced German air power at Dunkirk, proposed that capital ships should be camouflaged as, despite their size, information about them would be less easy to obtain.[4]

Meanwhile, in the autumn of 1940 Adm Dunbar-Nasmith, on his own initiative, commissioned the artist and naturalist Peter Scott to design a camouflage scheme for the ex-US Navy destroyers then coming under British command. Scott, also an amateur yachtsman, had joined the Royal Naval Volunteer Reserve and was now 1st lieutenant of the destroyer *Broke*, operating from Devonport. Applying his experience in observing birds to nautical matters, he appreciated that on starlit or cloudy nights the black silhouettes of ships were outlined against the sky from sea level. The obvious remedy was to paint the ships white but then by day they would be quickly spotted by searching aircraft. He therefore decided to paint the upper works and the upper part of the hull white and the lower part of the hull a very pale blue, the two colours meeting in a boldly serrated line. When observed from typical viewpoints of surface vessels the white areas would be seen against the sky and the blue against the rather darker tone of the sea. *Broke*'s camouflage was so effective that she twice became involved in collisions with other vessels.[5]

The Peter Scott or Western Approaches scheme took a little time to be accepted and to some extent this may have been owing to the artists at Leamington who, as already seen, were covering industrial buildings with disruptive patterns. It was not until late 1941 that the scheme became standard for all naval ships operating in the North

HMS *Broke* camouflaged with the Peter Scott or Western Approaches scheme
(*Imperial War Museum*)

Atlantic. By then a similar scheme had been applied to some capital ships and cruisers. When seen down light in bright sunlight the vessels shone like beacons so that the scheme was useless in, say, the Mediterranean. Eventually experiments with a telephotometer, which enables targets to be measured for their brightness at long range, confirmed Scott's theory. But at the time when the behaviour of light and vision against a background of sky and water had not yet been fully appreciated, it was a bold step to take.

At about the same time Capt Louis Mountbatten, then in command of the 5th Destroyer Flotilla, made unofficial experiments in painting his ships a curious pinkish grey tone rather like the gills of a mushroom.[6] This tone is believed to have been suggested by the ships of the Union-Castle Line painted pinkish-grey and difficult to see at dusk and dawn—the time when U-boats were most likely to attack. Actually Mountbatten Pink, as it was known to the British (but nipple pink to the Americans), was much more obvious than the Peter Scott scheme, ships painted in this colour being visible up to 8 miles as opposed to $5\frac{1}{2}$ in the latter scheme. The point was that tone rather than colour was important in camouflage.

One exception to this rule was explained by Schuil who was, it will be seen, to make important contributions to naval camouflage. This was the case of 'pure blue colours which have the property of appearing to have a lighter tone at night, due to a change in the spectral sensitivity of the eye at low levels of illumination, known as the Purkinje Effect. The amount of colouring in Mountbatten Pink,' continued Schuil, 'is barely enough to make this effect noticeable, but if it were effective it would make the tone appear darker at night than the corresponding grey tone.' Nevertheless, at the time, Mountbatten Pink was held to be highly effective and to the traditional

HMS *Rodney*. Note outlining of forward hull panels and the shadows cast by the barrels of 'A' turret. Similar shadows from 'B' turret would not be visible
(*Imperial War Museum*)

sailors it must have been almost as shocking as the white and blue of the Western Approaches scheme.

These 'unofficial' schemes made the Admiralty reverse its anti-camouflage policy. Hitherto such camouflage as there was had primarily been devised against air attack, but from February 1941 both surface and air attack were to be considered. 'From now on', minuted the Director of Operations (Home), 'all HM ships should be camouflaged and . . . the subject should be kept continually under review to produce the best designs.' Further policy laid down that first priority should be given to concealment and, secondly, to confusion of a ship's inclination and identity.[7]

Sea-going camouflage now became the responsibility of the Director of the Training and Staff Duties Division (DTSD), Capt (later Vice-Adm) J. W. Rivett-Carnac, succeeded as the war continued by Capt (later Vice-Adm) R. V. Symonds-Taylor and Capt H. P. K. Oram. Among a number of sections dealing with a variety of aspects of the war at sea, from torpedoes to Arctic clothing, was a camouflage section which included four RNVR officers, each with some kind of artistic training. They were Oliver Grahame-Hall, son of a Royal Academician and better known later in peace as Claude Muncaster, a marine and landscape painter who before the war had sailed before the mast in a windjammer; Robert Goodden, architect and industrial designer, later well-known for his Festival of Britain designs; David Pye, sculptor and woodcarver and later professor of furniture design at the Royal College of Art; and R. D. Russell, another architect and brother of Gordon Russell, the well-known designer, who became responsible for the camouflage of coastal forces.

The section had to state the requirement for the painting of every sea-going ship and vessel of the Fleet, and this meant a constant analysing of all the factors which affect the ease or difficulty with which a ship can be discerned in the conditions of weather and light in which she is most likely to be in contact with the enemy. It became clear to Capt R. Oliver-Bellasis, deputy director of DTSD, who had worked with scientists when dealing with magnetic mines, that it was essential to have a scientist to do this analysis. Consequently Alphonse Schuil, who had worked for the General Electric Co, and later H. Lang Brown were seconded to the division from the Directorate of Scientific Research to work on camouflage. Observations at sea (surface and air), reports from sea-going ships, interviews with officers on leave and laboratory experiments in simulated sea-going conditions provided the material for analysis. Further, a constant watch had to be kept on ships of new construction fitting out and ships refitting in dockyards between commissions to ensure that every ship and vessel was provided with the appropriate design before leaving dock for acceptance trials.

Horizontal surface painting of HMS *Nelson* in 1941. Deck is over-painted by dark grey and is matched by the turret tops and upper surfaces of the 16in barrels (*Imperial War Museum*)

After the Admiralty camouflage section had decided on how a ship should be painted, the naval section at Leamington worked out a design, sending a coloured drawing to the ship with a request that she be painted accordingly. The naval section was also responsible for the model tests in the viewing tank, which was capable of simulating most kinds of visibility and weather likely to be met.

Within about six months after enlisting scientific advice, a logical basis for the various visual phenomena had been found.[8] Selecting the right tone of paint for a particular condition of natural lighting was made possible by Schuil and his telephotometer. Before him, for instance, everyone had believed that white paint would only make a ship horribly conspicuous in moonlight, whereas Schuil proved that in certain conditions it would make a ship notably *in*conspicuous in moonlight.

The essence of the theory evolved by Schuil and his colleagues was that in diffused lighting conditions—overcast sky by day and night and in clear starlight—a ship could not be painted light enough: she needed to reflect 100 per cent of the light she received from the sky to match the tone of the sky, and white paint reflects less than 80 per cent. If seen against the sea near the horizon in these conditions she would have to be painted a very light grey, and a progressively darker grey as the angle of sighting moved towards the vertical (in the case of sighting by aircraft). When lit by the direct rays of the sun or moon, she would need to be painted rather dark grey. In this case the traditional grey of the Home Fleet, which had a 10 per cent reflection factor, was appropriate. Any and all of these tones increased rather than decreased her visibility in the wrong lighting conditions, so in determining the most suitable paint for any vessel it was necessary to pin-point the lighting conditions in which she would be operating most often, or in which it would be of the greatest value to her to escape notice, and paint her accordingly, accepting that in other conditions her visibility might be increased.

Obviously, at dawn and dusk, in darkness, or in haze or thick weather, any coat of paint—provided it was of a fairly neutral colour, whether lighter or darker—would reduce a ship's visibility. All the naval camoufleurs could do, therefore, was to apply paint of a suitable reflection factor to extend the variety of conditions of invisibility and to reduce the range slightly. This they sometimes achieved and since ships had to be painted anyway it was worthwhile trying to achieve it. Close attention had to be paid to the direction of light. In the even grey light of overcast cloud the paint must closely match the background of sea and sky. But when the sun comes out the situation changes, depending on the relation of the observer to the ship. If the sun is behind the ship she will be seen as a dark silhouette and no colour or tone of paint will do her any good. If the sun is behind the observer and therefore shining on the side of the ship which he sees, the ship's tone will be startlingly lighter and her colour, if appreciable at the range of sighting, much brighter. But, unlike an object on land which will reflect sunlight back to the observer, the sea with its glossy surface will usually reflect the sun's rays specularly, as a mirror does, directly away from the direction of the sun and away from the observer, and the atmosphere which forms the background of sky will transmit the sun's rays and not reflect them. Thus the ship which previously matched its background will now stand out against it as a bright intrusion.

Ideally, what the naval camoufleurs required was paint with the properties of a chameleon which would darken itself when lit by the direct rays of the sun or moon and lighten itself when under diffused light as from a monotonous grey sky. Several attempts were made to produce paint with variable tones. One was for submarines operating by night on the surface, in which chemical applications made white paint turn a darkish grey brown while a second application would restore the white. In another experiment an attempt was made to exploit the Purkinje Effect (the reaction of the eye to intense blue at night) by painting the cruiser *Berwick* this colour. Unfortunately this scheme was never given a proper chance as the disruptive scheme with which she was painted meant that only the darker areas of the pattern were painted in undiluted blue.

Disruptive camouflage was for the period 1942 to mid-1944 the order of the day, though the members of the Admiralty camouflage section came increasingly to believe that it was ineffective and that visibility could only be reduced on dark nights and at extreme range by day under an overcast sky. Three schemes were employed: light, dark and intermediate. The first was for northern climes; the second was appropriate in bright sunlight; and the third was intended for average conditions of haze, intermittent sun, cloud and moonlight.[9]

Countershading continued, of course, to be important. Deck areas where shadows were cast by guns, torpedo tubes, sponsons and bridge wings were painted white, fading out towards the edges. Sometimes very dense shadows were treated by adding a white reflective surface beneath them. The undersides of curved surfaces such as gun barrels, torpedo tubes and searchlights were painted a very light colour. The undersides of boats hung from davits were treated in a similar way. Masts were usually painted pure white as they were normally seen against the sky. In the Western Approaches the rear of the bridge was painted white.

A range of paints became available to carry out these schemes, each being given its own code number, indicating the tone value of the paint, and they were to be found in an Admiralty handbook. Tones ranging from black to light grey were represented by MS1 at the lower end of the scale to MS4—a very light grey. They could be mixed with shades of blue such as B5 and B6 to provide some colour. A range of grey tones was classified under the letter G, one of the most successful being G45, a light-grey tone.[10]

How useful was camouflage in the mists and high seas and long hours of darkness in the North Atlantic where the most crucial naval actions of the war were fought in defence of the Allied supply lines? Camouflage had to be looked at from a defensive and from an offensive point of view, from the air and from the surface of the sea.[11] The early stages of a convoy making for America or the Middle East were likely to be shadowed by reconnaissance aircraft. Here camouflage could do little because smoke could be seen from a distance of 60 miles, giving away the position of the convoy. The ships were then seen as dark dots silhouetted against the horizon; colour here was meaningless. Aircraft usually attacked at dusk or dawn; in the former event a white-painted ship was less conspicuous than one painted in grey. Ships showed up clearly in moonlight, but luckily the number of clear moonlit nights was well under half of the total hours of darkness.

U-boats, on the other hand, preferred to attack under the cloak of darkness. Using their torpedoes, they had to get within 5,000yd of the target, if possible closer, though when equipped with radar they could launch an attack from twice that range. However, for most of the war, the effectiveness of radar, hydrophones and sonar equipment was not such that it was possible to dispense with identifying the target visually. Therefore any means of making a convoy less conspicuous at night forced the U-boat to come closer to deliver its attack and thus make it more likely to be spotted and attacked by the

German cruiser in Norwegian fjord with dark ends and disruptive stripes. Note treatment of gun barrels of ship in foreground (*Public Record Office*)

escorts. Merchant ships were given away by their masts and funnels and in good visibility could be picked out as they came over the horizon. Generally speaking, it was easier for the submarine to see a target than for look-outs to spot the submarine. In a crow's nest, for instance, there was usually only one pair of eyes compared to several on the bridge of a U-boat.

The escorting vessel had to remain inconspicuous for as long as possible as the U-boat approached. As one of Goodeve's scientists put it:

> The difference in time between [the] escort seeing a U-boat and the U-boat seeing the escort may make all the difference between a successful counter-attack with at least a detractive value if not actual contact, and a tardy attempt to prevent something which has already taken place.[12]

At night the silhouette had to be reduced as far as possible. While the use of white narrowed the range of visibility, Graham Kerr's idea of diminishing the outline with direct or diffused lighting was revived. If the brightness of the ship could be controlled with a rheostat so that it always matched its background, this would be the perfect camouflage. The most suitable type of vessel on which to install direct lighting was a destroyer or corvette when homing on a U-boat after a radar contact or high-frequency/direction-finding bearing. If the hunter ship could avoid a silhouette, the U-boat would be deprived of its advantage of seeing without being seen.

Experiments were made by Canadian scientists under Prof E. G.

Characteristic camouflage for US Navy destroyer, 1944 (*Public Record Office*)

Burr in mid-1943 using the destroyer HMCS *Edmundston*. About fifty lamps were mounted on outriggers facing forward, which could be swung in or out quite easily by one of the crew. The stowage of the equipment meant the loss of twenty light and fifteen heavy depth charges. Although the experiments worked quite well at short ranges, the expense and difficulties of supplying and operating the equipment was believed to be prohibitive.[13] In any case British surface radar was by then improving rapidly.

Another proposal for protecting convoys at night was by emitting smoke screens.[14] Again, this could only provide cover as long as the submarine crew had to rely on visual contact to sink a ship. Some 450 merchantmen were fitted out with smoke-laying apparatus. Each vessel was capable of emitting smoke from one to four nozzles. Even with a wind it was possible to conceal at least three sides of a convoy.

Smoke was more valuable in conditions of poor visibility, especially on moonless or overcast moonlit nights. Provided the screening vessels were hidden from view, smoke could prevent a deliberate attack from being made on a convoy. It would not, however, reduce the effectiveness of acoustic weapons such as the German 'Gnat' torpedo.

By the end of 1943 the battle of the Atlantic had been won and there was little prospect of large-scale surface engagements with the German Navy. By then doubts about the value of disruptive camouflage had been confirmed, particularly on receipt of a report made by Grahame-Hall after a prolonged tour of the Mediterranean, South Atlantic and Indian Ocean. The purpose of his tour was, firstly, to observe meteorological conditions and levels of light illumination as they affected sea-going camouflage; and, secondly, to arrange trials from the air and surface and subsequently to advise commanders-in-chief of foreign stations on the best camouflage for the prevailing conditions and tactical requirements. Grahame-Hall took Schuil with him to make the observations while he arranged the trials.[15]

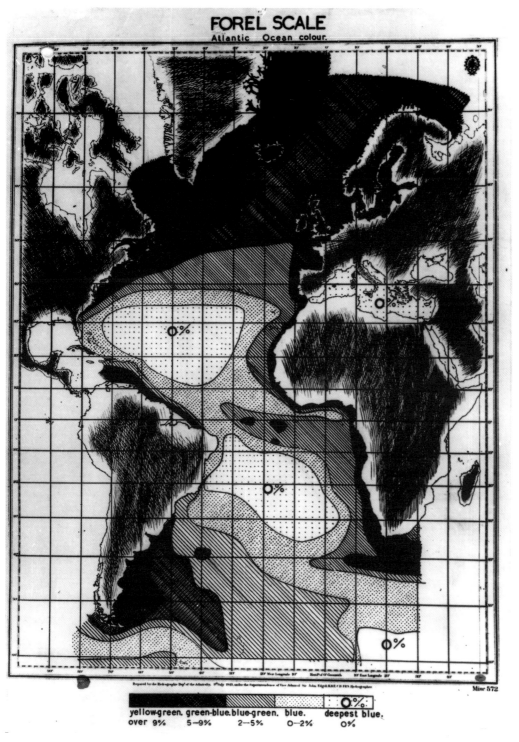

FOREL SCALE
Atlantic Ocean colour.

yellow-green.	green-blue.	blue-green.	blue.	deepest blue.
over 9%	5–9%	2–5%	0–2%	0%

Scale of colours in North and South Atlantic indicating the various backgrounds against which a warship might be observed (*Public Record Office*)

This combination was tragically broken when Schuil, who had temporarily parted company to make observations from a submarine, was killed when the latter was torpedoed by a U-boat off Freetown, Grahame-Hall apparently being the only person to witness it. In his report Grahame-Hall pointed out that camouflage would only give positive results before dawn and after dusk from sea surface level. He quoted Schuil as having noted that conditions favouring concealment seldom occurred. Even in optimum conditions reduction of the visible range was not great and the presence of pattern hardly affected visible range.

The other factor which had far-reaching effects on the value of camouflage was the improved performance of radar. Indeed some senior naval officers, notably the Vice-Admiral Commanding North Atlantic Station, questioned whether the policy of reducing visibility should not be abandoned and a return made to the old idea of causing confusion.[16] But this argument was rejected by the Admiralty on the grounds that the design would be essentially the same, only larger in pattern, and that radar had not yet (1942) 'turned night into day'.

Reduction of visibility therefore remained first priority for naval vessels until the end of the war. By then they were painted light grey, but with a blue panel on the hull. In daylight the light grey tended to offset the shadows cast by projections of the superstructure and the blue panels gave a foreshortening effect to confuse judgement of inclination. This compromise between the two theories of camouflage was used in all zones of operation and was only modified for special types of vessel such as convoy escorts and aircraft carriers.

Some naval authorities would no doubt argue that sea-going camouflage was a waste of time. On the other hand, it could justifiably be said that although camouflage had no spectacular achievement to its credit, the progress made with the reduction of a ship's visibility in certain conditions justified the activity and the relatively modest use of manpower and resources. An appropriately painted ship would escape detection at extreme sighting range for a little longer than an inappropriately painted one. That could enable her to get a first shot in before the enemy and might sometimes save her from submarine attack altogether. Both were important advantages.[17]

Before we turn to other aspects of sea-going camouflage, note should be taken of how the Americans were dealing with the problem. In mid-1940 naval technical development became the responsibility of the Bureau of Ships (BuShips), which set up a research and development branch for sea-going camouflage. BuShips laid down the colours to be painted on both vertical and deck surfaces. Whereas the Admiralty never gave orders but provided information to commanders-in-chief and ships' captains, in certain cases requesting them to take action, the Americans actually issued instructions, though some small

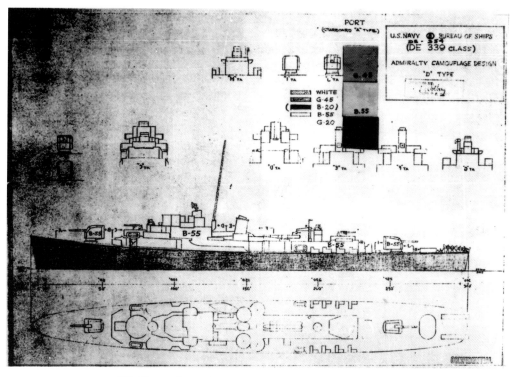

PORT
(STARBOARD 'A' TYPE)

WHITE
G·45
(B·20)
B·55
G·20

US Navy scheme for destroyer based on Admiralty design
(*Public Record Office*)

craft seem to have been allowed much more latitude. These schemes
were known as Measures and were given code numbers. They reflected
the colours prevailing in the different hemispheres of operation.

For amphibious operations in the South-West Pacific many small
ships operated close inshore against a jungle background and were
largely painted dark green and brown. In deep water, dark greys and
blues merging with the deep blue of the sea helped to provide concealment from the air. Again, like the British, the Americans used
disruptive patterns especially in the Pacific, where it was necessary to
confuse the aim of submarines and aircraft. On occasion dark colours
were used to change the appearance of the class of ship or to reduce
the visibility of some of its armaments. Decks of aircraft carriers·were
hard to conceal and at first were painted dark grey, later being painted
sea blue or navy blue.

The Admiralty, and DMWD was the department concerned, was
also involved in inshore operations off the Norwegian coast. Motor
torpedo boats would penetrate a fjord, moor against a cliff and wait
until an opportunity arose for them to emerge and attack a German
coastal convoy. Camouflage was essential for all stages of the operation, but the lying-up period was particularly dangerous as the craft
could be spotted by searching aircraft or surface patrols.[18]

Currie, of DMWD, devised nets to enable the boats to merge into
the sides of the cliff. One side was suitable for siting against a back-

Umbrella camouflage for British coastal craft lying up against cliff
(*Public Record Office*)

ground of rocks and vegetation and the reverse was·garnished with white patches for the same background covered with snow. When tested, the nets were found to be too heavy. Smaller ones were made and the white patches were rolled up in a separate bundle and could be attached to the nets by lanyards.

These special nets covered the gap between the cliff and the boat, the deck and sides of the latter being covered by standard army camouflage nets. The boat itself was painted with land camouflage colours of black, green and dark brown. A feature which would arouse curiosity was the long unbroken line of the boat's hull. Outriggers were therefore erected to hold the nets away from the sides.

Similar raiding operations took place around the islands of the Aegean, which are often studded with small rocky inlets. To suit the different climate and landscape, nets known as Indian Open Weave, made of loosely woven fabric of a small mesh, were used. They were kept off the superstructure by bamboo poles fitted with round discs at the top made of wire-netting so they would not damage the mesh. In the latter stage of the war, when the air threat had disappeared, the emphasis was transferred from land concealment to the reduction of visibility at sea.

A picturesque alternative to the concealment of MTBs by netting was suggested by the Admiralty camouflage section. On arrival at their proposed hide after an exhausting and perhaps nerve-racking journey, the crew were usually in no mood to drape nets over their craft—a time-consuming business. It might be made easier if they had large umbrellas consisting of patches of colour which could be raised or lowered as required. However, the umbrellas had to be secured by numerous guys and lashings criss-crossing the deck and it requires little imagination to appreciate the inconvenience, not to mention the injury, that could be caused when having to move about at night. This scheme consequently never went beyond the trial stage.

Another type of hazardous operation which required concealment at very close range was the limpet attacks on enemy vessels (involving the fixing of explosives to the hull) and carried out by a crew of two paddling a canoe.[19] These tiny craft had to be inconspicuous both during the approach to and right up against the side of the target. This meant they had to be painted light to render them less visible at a distance but had to look darker when directly below an observer looking over the side of a vessel rising up some 25ft above the water level. The problem was thus how to provide dark and light colours almost simultaneously. After lengthy trials, a number of which were conducted on a reservoir at Staines, Currie, who was well acquainted with the problems of a marine artist, found that a shiny black provided a slightly better protection than a dull black or a blue at all the distances required. The bottoms of the canoes were painted in land-camouflage colours and face-veil netting was used to cover them when beached.

Great care had to be taken to conceal the crews and the shine from faces, paddles or hands had to be eliminated. Currie invented a light-grey smock, known as an 'octopus suit', provided with a hood which, together with the arms and shoulders, were covered with brown patches to reduce visibility.

The intention was that the canoes, to be used in Far-Eastern waters, should be launched from submersible 'mother craft', known as mobile floating units. They would lie on the sea-bed until required to return to base with their canoes. A suitable colouring had to be given them while in this position which might be against a background of dark, grey-green mud, light-yellow sand, or white coral. Experiments in a London swimming bath, using special lighting equipment, ended in the decks being painted a sandy colour and the slab-like shape of the hull was broken up by light and dark shading.

From the beginning of the war, merchant ships sailed in convoy and were not dazzle-painted as they had been in late 1917–18. But when it was noted that the funnels and superstructures painted in light colours such as red, buff and white stood out when sunlit against the sombre background of quays and warehouses, the question was asked what would happen when they were seen against the usual grey background of clouds and sky at sea?[20] From April 1941, after experiments by DMWD, they were painted in two standard grey colours, one covering the sides and vertical surfaces called Merchant Ship Side (MSS) and a slightly darker colour known as Merchant Ship Deck (MSD).

In 1943 after the Western Approaches scheme had proved its worth and analysis had revealed not only that about 67 per cent of attacks on merchant shipping were made in twilight, darkness, or when the moon was rising or had risen, but that the highest proportion of shipping sunk was above Lat 35°N, or the North Atlantic, there was a case for lightening merchant ship grey to an even greater extent. This colour was called Light MSS; deck camouflage remained the same. Top masts and funnels were painted white, making a hull-down ship much less easy to see.

Aerial observation by Currie showed that when merchant ships were painted with a high-gloss paint they became very conspicuous at dawn and dusk when illuminated against a rising or setting sun, and when seen against a low bank of cloud. Using a gloss-measuring instrument devised by the Paint Research Station at Teddington, paints were produced which toned down to a matt surface shortly after being applied. This meant, of course, that the quality of the paint suffered and ships had to be repainted more frequently. However, by late 1942 sea-going officers attached less importance to the need to tone down glossy paint than in the past.

Some fast ships, like the *Queen Mary* and *Queen Elizabeth*, travelled independently, and it was proposed that they should be painted with the Western Approaches colour scheme, though sunlight would make them more, rather than less, conspicuous.[21] But there was no unanimous view about this problem. Some submarine officers suggested that the high percentage of night attacks might be the result of merchant ships being shadowed by day, the U-boats closing in on their victims at night, selecting the best time for attack. In the end the chiefs of staff held that camouflage in clear daylight conditions made no difference, but in poor visibility or at night, it might cause the enemy to make an incorrect estimation of the course of his target.

Structural camouflage, or disguise, was also employed, not only on naval vessels in order to confuse identification, but also on merchant vessels. This work was the responsibility of the Admiralty camouflage section. Tankers were extremely easy to identify by their silhouette and, because of their precious cargo, were favourite targets of the U-boats. They were therefore disguised as 'three-island'-superstructure merchant ships, which enabled them to escape being singled out for attack at night. Pye, who was closely involved with merchant-ship camouflage, recalls that it was important to make the dummy funnel amidships very large as earlier attempts by the Ministry of War Transport had been unconvincing.

Disguise was also used in certain combined operations, notably for the Dieppe Raid, in order to confuse the enemy's defences.

Although the British quickly abandoned the decoy ships, to which so much publicity had been given in the inter-war period, and the US Navy, not long after entering the war, followed suit because the casualties incurred did not compensate for the number of submarines destroyed, the Germans met with a measure of success in this kind of deception.[22] In the course of the war fewer than a dozen German raiders *(Hilfskreuzer)* destroyed or captured 138 ships, including a British armed merchant cruiser, and sank the *Sydney*, an Australian cruiser, while they escorted thirty prizes back to German or Japanese bases. In doing so they drew off warships otherwise urgently engaged in blockade or anti-U-boat operations. They would doubtless have caused greater damage had not the wireless traffic between them and their headquarters been intercepted and deciphered and the appropriate action taken because of the remarkable British intelligence and deciphering organisation.

As in World War I, the armaments had to be invisible at close quarters and especially from aerial observation. Guns were hidden in folding deck houses or behind false bulwarks. Others were installed below weather-decks where their location depended as much upon the contouring of the ship as upon naval requirements. They had to be capable of going into action instantly.

The crews had to remain unobserved for long periods, which imposed a strain on their morale, though there was some compensation when the ship put into a neutral port for fresh provisions. Not only were quantities of stores required, but tons of paint and bulky structural materials were necessary to make the frequent changes of disguise. In order to accommodate the large crews, in the event of having to abandon ship, rubber boats were stowed away out of sight as too many lifeboats would have aroused suspicion.

The development of camouflage for aircraft in flight bears a remarkable similarity to the changes in policy for sea-going camouflage. As at sea, variations in the background (in this case changes in light resulting from clouds, mist, haze, or sun) meant that one form of camouflage never suited all conditions, and it was obviously impracticable to keep changing schemes to suit particular conditions.

In World War I aircraft usually flew at low levels over a landscape scarred with craters and trench systems on tasks for the Army. For most of the war camouflage of aircraft by the British was either discouraged or conducted on an unscientific basis. The possibility of air operations much further behind the front and night attacks on targets in Germany and the need to counter German night-bomber attacks on England led to experiments in reducing the visibility of day- and night-flying aircraft at Martlesham Heath. A little later valuable studies were carried out by M. Luckiesh, a physicist employed by the General Electric Co in America and who was then chairman of a camouflage committee of the National Research Council. He appreciated the need for different colours for upper and lower surfaces of the aircraft and the importance of non-reflecting paint on night-flying aircraft. He anticipated that white paint might be less conspicuous against a moonlit sky than black.

When aircraft were camouflaged for operations over the Western Front, irregular patches were painted on surfaces in the form of curves or stripes running diagonally over the fuselage. They were intended to harmonise with the landscape below and were generally brown and earth green. Vertical surfaces were painted in a lighter colour to counteract the shadow cast by the top wing (most aircraft at that time having two wings).

After the war the Royal Aircraft Establishment at Farnborough became responsible for designing camouflage schemes for all types of aircraft. It was the only service research establishment to take a serious interest in camouflage in the inter-war period.[23] This work was the responsibility of the chemistry department on account of its knowledge of the paints and dopes used on aircraft surfaces. Among others, five scientific officers should be mentioned in advising on camouflage before and during the war. They were Dr J. E. Ramsbottom, then head of the department, and Dr J. O. Hughes, who was concerned with tropical camouflage. As Gilbert Palmer, who—it has been seen—reintroduced camouflage to the Army, became involved at Leamington and in London, the technical side was taken over by Dr J. D. Main-Smith who had come to Farnborough after successful careers in the academic world and in industry. With his assistant, E. C. Jones, he made important contributions not only to in flight camouflage but to problems of texture, reflectivity and the early work on infra-red camouflage.

Urgent instructions to RAE during the Abyssinian crisis in October 1935 led to Jones working through the night marking out chalk patterns on every RAE aircraft while all available junior staff followed him with cans of dope and brushes. According to a colleague, although perhaps not a first-class painting job, on a misty morning the results were quite impressive. Subsequently these designs were tested by RAF aircraft and experiments were made with flying-boats and seaplanes at Calshot on the Solent.

By 1936 the principles of aircraft camouflage had been established.[24] In temperate climates (Europe) the predominant colours are the green of vegetation and the brown of the soil. Upper surfaces of aircraft were therefore painted in two standard colours—'dark green' and 'dark earth'. In tropical countries (including the Middle East) the schemes were usually pairs of colours, 'dark earth' and 'light earth', or 'dark sand' and 'dark red'. For maritime aircraft in temperate climates the predominant colours are the blue and grey green of deep and shallow water. Here 'extra-dark sea grey' and 'dark slate grey' were the standard colours. In tropical seas the green predom-

Low-flying Whitley bomber with disruptive painting enabling it to merge into the countryside beneath it (*Imperial War Museum*)

inate and the standard colours were 'dark Mediterranean blue' and 'extra-dark sea green'.

These combinations of colours were intended for upper surfaces and effectively reduced visibility from above and when the aircraft was at rest on the ground. Under-surface camouflage was applied without pattern so as to make the aircraft hard to spot against a day sky background. In temperate climates a light duck-egg blue ('standard sky') was applied to aircraft operating over land and sea by day at, or near, cloud level. In the Middle East under surfaces were painted a dark sky blue ('standard azure blue'). Much research went into discovering the best camouflage for night bombers, as will be seen, the main problem being to reduce reflection from searchlight beams. At the outset of the war they were painted black on the sides and lower surfaces and the upper surfaces were rendered dark green and brown. Matt paint was applied in all cases to reduce glint and reflection.

Aircraft paint was, of course, not only required to reduce visibility, but also to protect the aircraft, tauten surfaces, to identify it and, in special cases, to help it to move faster. For these reasons paint had to be applied with great care in a draught- and dust-free atmosphere and in a temperature which did not allow the formation of moisture cooled by the vaporisation of the solvent. Constant maintenance was necessary to keep surfaces free from dirt and oil.

The camouflage schemes described above were tested in the Battle of Britain, the beginning of the night-bomber offensive against Germany, and the increasingly vital part played by the air in anti-U-boat patrols. By the spring of 1941 the time had come for a reappraisal of camouflage and several innovations were made in the light of recent experience.

A new type of operation in which camouflage was the principal form of protection, apart from speed and ability to climb to high altitudes, was strategic photographic reconnaissance, made at first by unarmed Spitfires with range extended by Mosquitos in the summer of 1941. At the outset of war Wing-Cdr Sydney Cotton, a non-conforming outsider who, on his own initiative, had organised the first reconnaissance flights over military and naval targets in Germany, had painted the underside of his special aircraft a duck-egg green called Camotint.[25] This colour was claimed to make the aircraft virtually invisible at heights of around 10,000ft. But by 1941 improved types of Spitfire were flying at altitudes of over 40,000ft. At these heights, when viewed above the clouds, the colour of the sky changes from light to a dark blue as the altitude increases, appearing a deep purple on the threshold of the stratosphere. (The reason for the sky becoming darker is a reduction in the thickness of the atmosphere directly overhead.) A darker blue was therefore required. Pilots believed that the most suitable tone lay between 'standard sky blue' and 'standard light Mediterranean blue' and in August 1941 the new colour was named 'deep sky blue'. The finish had to be as matt as was consistent with speed to eliminate light reflected from the fuselage or the cowling. The white of the roundels was deleted as it gave away the aircraft at practically all angles of sight. The preliminary investigations for this new colour were made by Prof Merton, last encountered in connection with research on smoke.

At about this time the Operational Research Section (ORS) at Headquarters, Coastal Command, a band of lively and inquisitive scientists and engineers led by the well-known physicist Patrick Blackett, himself capable of reducing a tactical problem to its essentials in the same way as he analysed a laboratory experiment, was investigating the technical aspects of air–sea operations. One of its first tasks had been to discover why U-boats were diving before patrol aircraft were able to attack them.[26] This was because look-outs in the conning-tower of the submarine always saw the aircraft against the sky. Whether the latter was cloudy or clear, the observer invariably saw the lower surface, which was usually darker than its background. In the Western Approaches, aircraft generally moved against an overcast sky with no direct sunlight. Under such conditions the lower surfaces were illuminated by light reflected from the sea, which is about one-twentieth the intensity of light from the sky. Even if the aircraft reflected 100 per cent of the light falling on it, it would still appear dark against its background.

In addition to the maritime aircraft painted 'blue sea grey' Coastal Command was employing bomber aircraft, such as Whitleys, painted black. As a result of several reports written by a young physicist, W. R. Merton, it was decided to paint the underside and vertical sides of such aircraft a matt white for a trial period from September 1941. By the end of the year the ORS had prepared a definitive scheme which was accepted by the commander-in-chief and put into general use. The scheme allowed for three different roles: one was for night, when searchlights might be encountered for which the aircraft were painted black; two were for normal sea patrols. In the two latter cases all surfaces which could be seen from vertically beneath the aircraft were painted a glossy white, the side surfaces which could be seen from the U-boat were painted matt white and the upper surfaces remained the normal grey. In the Mediterranean the sides of maritime aircraft were painted dark sea grey against the strong sunlight.

The ORS then tried to evaluate the effect the new camouflage had on the effectiveness of anti-U-boat patrols. One calculation showed that over a wide range of visibilities a white aircraft should be able to approach about 20 per cent nearer with the same likelihood of being spotted as a black one. Another estimate suggested that this might lead to about 40 per cent more U-boats being sighted before they themselves spotted the aircraft and dived; and the number of U-boats attacked on the surface was expected to increase even more. In the event, because of the deteriorating standards of training of U-boat crews the figures proved to be even higher than anticipated.

At the time an improvement of 20 per cent was not good enough and other suggestions were made to reduce visibility. One of these was the artificial illumination of the aircraft to enable it to harmonise with its background in the same way as the diffused lighting tried out on the *Edmundston* described earlier. But this arrangement proved to be very expensive in power, requiring about 40kW alone for a Whitley bomber fuselage. The Americans then took over the idea and revised it so that the lighting was used only for roughly head-on views—more practical a proposition as most sightings were made of targets near the nose, and this was usually the part of the aircraft turned towards the U-boat during the run-in to attack. The scheme, known as 'Yahoody the Impossible', might have been employed in strikes against enemy shipping when it would perhaps have confused the enemy anti-aircraft gunners. But the war ended before it could be put into practice.

During the Battle of Britain, fought in the skies over southern England with its brown and green landscape, the temperate land scheme covering the Hurricanes and Spitfires undoubtedly helped the defenders during those critical summer weeks. The glint of the sun and light reflections on polished surfaces had strenuously to be avoided and shortly after the battle instructions were issued that a matt finish should be applied to Spitfires.[27] (At that time, because of the need for dispersal on airfields and the lack of manpower for servicing, the surface polishing necessary to gain maximum speed was difficult to achieve.) Not long afterwards, the upper-surface camouflage of day-fighters was lightened because of the increased altitudes at which interceptions were taking place.

By the summer of 1942, however, Fighter Command had moved over to the offensive and was engaging the enemy on the far side of the Channel. In order to be inconspicuous against the sea as well as the land day-fighters were painted dark green and ocean grey on their upper surfaces and medium sea grey underneath. Improved German fighter performance, particularly the FW190, severely tested the capability of the British fighters. Even an increase in speed of 3 to 5mph could influence the outcome of an aerial combat. The decision was taken, after requests by Sholto Douglas, commander of Fighter Command, to rescind the ruling on a matt finish even though aircraft would become more conspicuous. Greater attention to smoothing the wing surfaces and body of the Spitfire and to cleaning it in general increased its speed by about 5mph.

British night-fighters were engaged only in an intercepting role during the Blitz and the spasmodic night raids against targets in southern England that occurred later in the war. During the Blitz they were painted black all over. Interceptions usually took place on moonless nights and it was discovered that when they were operating above 20,000ft they became more conspicuous. Tests initiated by No 85 Beaufighter Squadron, then commanded by Wing-Cdr Peter Townsend, showed that, when their upper surfaces were painted dark green and medium sea green and medium sea grey for underneath, they were much harder to see against the background, usually dark-grey cloud or the earth which at that altitude appeared blue or green in tone because of mist or haze. This scheme superseded the all-black.[28]

German camouflage schemes varied little from the British and at about the same time as Fighter Command changed over to its new night-fighter scheme, their German counterparts adopted a mixture of brown, green and blue. One of their leading night-fighter pilots, Maj Stieb, flew an aircraft that was almost white on top. British night-fighter pilots were also known to devise their own schemes. Instructions had been given that 'special night', described below, should be given priority over durability and ease of application. E. C. Jones, sent to check on whether these instructions were being obeyed, found at North Weald a pilot seated on a stool painting his aircraft

dark grey speckled with white. It looked like a speckled hen and he explained that this was how an aircraft looked in moonlight. Since he wished to be invisible to the enemy rather than to a friendly searchlight crew, I conceded that his scheme could be as good or even better than 'special night' and we parted without rancour.

Later in the war camouflage of night-fighters took second place to performance, as with day-fighters. When the matt colour of the Mosquito, for example, was removed, its speed was increased by as much as 15mph.[29]

The night-bomber offensive against Germany was probably the grimmest, most hard-fought campaign of the war and the high casualty rate of air crew not unlike that associated with the bloody offensives of the Western Front in 1914–18. Indeed at one point in early 1944 casualties to aircraft were approaching 10 per cent, the figure generally agreed sufficient to stop the campaign. Casualties were reduced by radio countermeasures, such as the dropping of metal foil, called Window, and in the end a special group devoted itself to the jamming of ground and air-borne radar, but these operations cannot be included in a study of visual camouflage.

Darkness by itself was inadequate to provide cover for the bombers. Even without a moon it is possible on most nights to observe an aircraft at a distance of 1,000ft from another machine. Similarly, depending on whether or not there is moonlight or cloud, the number of nights an aircraft can be seen from the ground at a height of 1,000ft is surprisingly high. No satisfactory camouflage for night-bombers was evolved because so many factors had to be taken into account on an operational flight.[30] Visibility varied according to whether there was moonlight or not, cloud, haze, or mist, and so long as the enemy was likely to attack home bases, consideration had to be given to the bombers standing on the ground in the day. These factors were also influenced by the height of operation, the territory over which the bombers were flying, and the relation between the weather and the scale of attack.

Moreover, a camouflage which might be suitable against night-fighters would make the aircraft show up in searchlights. In general, as the war progressed, fighters were responsible for bringing more aircraft down than guns (in 1942 it was about 55 per cent as opposed to 30 per cent and this ratio increased as radar improved). Again, throughout the war one type of bomber had a higher loss rate than the others. At one time it was the Stirling, then it was the Halifax. There were, of course, a variety of reasons for losses apart from camouflage deficiencies, varying from performance to the experience of the crews.

In spite of such difficulties, an attempt to camouflage the night-bomber had to be made and the painting of upper and lower surfaces had their own distinctive problems. In the case of the former the tone had to match a dark cloud or ground background. In the early days of the war aircraft were painted black all over. But it was found that the reflectivity of the background varied according to the density of the cloud. According to a Bomber Command operational researcher, in normal dense cloud '40–65 per cent of the incidental light [could] be reflected, but from dense cloud of great depth the proportion may be of 75 per cent and from thin cloud 35–40 per cent.' Usually the bombers flew above cloud, where the amount of reflection was about 50 per cent. Ideally, a very pale matt finish, possibly white and pale grey, was the most suitable but, because of the complications described above, black was generally preferred for upper surfaces. Owing to the inability of the experts to guarantee improvements in existing camouflage schemes, bomber groups tended to adopt schemes they believed suited them. One group might retain the original dark green and earth which, though slightly inferior to black, at least had the advantage of being less visible by day. Another group would prefer dark green and grey; and at one time No 4 Group painted its Whitleys black all over, the object being to increase the matt colour rather than to intensify the black. At least disruptive patterns were not approved for in the dark it is impossible to distinguish between colours : tone was all-important.

Concealment of lower surfaces was primarily designed to reduce the reflection from searchlights. Prof N. F. (later Sir Nevill) Mott, another distinguished physicist working for the Army Operational Research Group on the theory of searchlight illumination early in 1943, was struck by the decrease in range when the diffuse reflection from a bomber was as low as 3 per cent. He suggested to Dr Dickins, head of Bomber Command Operational Research Section, that it might be better to concentrate on improving camouflage than on taking evasive action.

About that time the scientists at RAE had been instructed to find a black which was blacker than the 'standard black' invented by Prof Merton and which he claimed 'reflected three quarters of 1 per cent of the incident light, regardless of the angle of incidence'.[31] After examining a number of carbon-black pigments one was received which, applied in a shellac medium, gave a velvety black finish far superior to 'standard night'. When examined under the microscope, the pigment was seen to be spores of lycopodium dyed black. As there was not enough lycopodium powder to supply the needs of Bomber Command an alternative had to be found. The nearest pigment to it was Monolite Fast Black, an ICI product applied in an ethyl cellulose medium. But, Dr Jones recalls,

> petroleum hydrocarbons were hard to come by, being earmarked for military use. I spent hours walking on the perimeter tracks of East Anglian airfields because no fuel was available for transport, but at Farnborough common sense prevailed. 'Special Night' was formulated with high octane aviation spirit and no questions were asked.

It had been hoped that 'special night' would be less conspicuous than

Illustration of tone values on night bombers above and below horizon by
Roy Nockolds (*Public Record Office*)

'standard black' when a bomber was held by searchlights, but trials
with the two colours were inconclusive.

If anything, aircraft painted 'standard night' were more difficult to
follow by visually controlled searchlights than 'special night' and the
former was adopted by Bomber Command.

The following July a report by the aircraft artist, Roy Nockolds,
and Ian McRitchie from RAE, concluded that night-bombers were
being painted too dark and that their silhouettes were blacker and
more obvious than their background.[32] This could be vital when the
pilot was taking evasive action, turning, climbing or diving. If fighters
were trying to intercept at a height of between 8,000 and 20,000ft
and the bomber was seen slightly below the horizon, its background
was at least 10 miles away. Nockolds and McRitchie concluded that
flat under surfaces should be painted a shiny black, curved under
surfaces a matt black and the upper surface a special pattern of light
grey.

Experiments with three aircraft painted either black, with a white
under surface, or with a shiny black under surface, confirmed that the
best colour for the under surface was still black, but whether it should
be glossy or matt was still undecided as occasionally the aircraft
painted matt was not held continuously by the beams, even when the
bomber was flying straight and level.

Comparisons in trials by the Americans also indicated that glossy
black was preferable to matt and the ORS tried to persuade staff
officers of Bomber Command to appreciate its merits. But the latter,
who had operational experience, remained unconvinced on the
grounds that shiny aircraft coned by multiple searchlight beams were
bound to be more obvious than matt-painted machines because of the
very bright reflections from the surfaces in such conditions. Moreover
at night, 'silhouettes play such an important part and the conditions

and intensity of light vary to such an extent that any practicable scheme is ineffective.'[33] Matt black was therefore retained for the remainder of the war.

Night-flying aircraft could be spotted by the identification roundels painted in yellow, blue, white and red on the side of the fuselage and the vertical yellow and blue flash on the tail. The white and yellow rings had a high reflectivity rate. Yellow had been introduced as a means of identifying aircraft when camouflaged and, after Dunkirk, of making a distinction from identical types of aircraft which had fallen into the hands of the Germans. Maj R. J. Leeds, a Territorial Army searchlight officer who, on account of his scientific background, had joined the Operational Research Group of the Air Defence Research and Development Establishment, was, in June 1941, the first to point out that whereas the German bombers had the swastika emblem partially obliterated by black paint, British roundels, according to reports, appeared as 'bright lights' when picked out by search-lights.[34] Bomber squadrons, on their own initiative, took to obscuring the white and yellow circles. It was decided that the yellow rings should not be omitted. The problem of reducing the size of the colours was passed to RAE. According to Dr Jones, a solution was found based on the fact that the resolving power of the eye is limited.

> There is a minimum angle which a shape must subtend at the eye if it is to be clearly seen. A circular disc divided into red, white, blue and yellow areas can be made to disappear against the surface on which it is painted at any specified distance. The shape, size, pattern and colouring of the roundel had already been decided; we were free to recommend changes in the width of the rings and the tone of the colours. Our recommendations were accepted.

The vertical strip in the flash on the tail was also narrowed. The new regulations came into force in April 1942, the policy supporting them being that markings should become visible as soon as the silhouette of the aircraft could be recognised as a particular type under average conditions of weather and background.

A natural hazard that revealed bombers flying over enemy defences was hoar frost forming on the wings and which shone in the searchlights. De-icing fluid and apparatus for heating the wing through exhaust from the engines were solutions put forward to meet this problem.[35]

At one point, early in the war, it was thought that the Germans were using infra-red telescopes to detect the exhaust rings of the British bombers. The antidote was temporarily to paint a high temp-erature anti-infra-red paint on the exhausts and, more permanently, to design a shield for the exhaust system.

8 CONCEALING AGAINST THE INVISIBLE

> The need for cover, the need to conceal from the enemy strength
> and movement, and hence intention, persists.
>
> Gen A. Farrar Hockley, *Adelphi*
> *Paper No 144*, 1978

Since the end of the 1950s radical changes have occurred in the technique of conventional warfare. Manned aircraft like the American U2—infamous after Gary Powers was shot down by the Russians, thus precipitating the failure of the Paris summit meeting—can photograph objects on the ground from heights of 100,000ft so that they can be recognised by even the untrained eye. Objects less than 1ft long may be photographed by observation satellites and other types of remotely piloted vehicles flying 100 miles above the surface of the earth. Sideways-looking radar makes it possible for satellites to operate in all kinds of weather. The ability to fly at great altitudes and speed enables such vehicles to operate secretly and continuously in peace time.[1]

While the conventional aerial camera is still cheaper and more flexible to operate, other forms of sensor, able to penetrate darkness, smoke or mist, have become available to the gatherer of battlefield intelligence. Infra-red cameras, in their infancy in World War II, can now be used with conventional or special films registering colour or black-and-white images in ultra-violet or near-infra-red bandwidths. Television cameras mounted on masts or in the nose of remotely piloted vehicles can observe the battlefield continuously without exposing the observer on the ground to danger. Lasers provide a source of light or infra-red radiation which illuminate the object under study with a highly concentrated beam. New systems of infra-red detection have replaced, or are replacing, earlier devices which could operate only with the assistance of an infra-red searchlight and were liable to detection and interference themselves. The new passive sensors have the advantage of being optically undetectable and easy to handle. Thermal cameras producing pictures on a cathode-ray tube like a TV picture register heat radiation from vehicles and helicopters and are used for observation at night. They are able to look sideways as well as forward, but are handicapped in cloud and rain. Electronic image-intensifiers used at night make pictures in the near-infra-red spectrum 50,000 times brighter than the original. The improved picture may then be transmitted optically to cameras or television for presentation.[2]

A number of these new methods of detection were stimulated by the Vietnam War. The ease with which the North Vietnam army and the Viet Cong melted into the forest or undergrowth made them able to defy technically superior forces and the American airpower operating in support of the South Vietnamese. Much of the Viet Cong's success against the Americans has been attributed to the elaborate tunnel systems, begun when they were fighting the French and by 1966 extending for 150 miles. They were used for some of the most daring operations of the war—such as the raid on the US Embassy in Saigon in January 1968, marking the beginning of the Tet offensive—until the final assault on Saigon in March 1975. Sometimes, while crouching in these tunnels, the Viet Cong could hear American officers talking and scraping their chairs overhead.

The Americans retaliated by using dogs and then 'tunnel rats'—hand-picked men, small in stature, who attempted to eject their enemies with explosives and gas, but this led only to the excavation of alternative tunnels and the building of trap-doors as protection against blast and gas. Seismic detectors were used with limited success.

Much of the fighting took place at night on the surface, the Americans being helped by the latest detection devices. Targets were located by infra-red equipment mounted on helicopters, while on the ground snipers obtained accuracy with infra-red searchlight and star-light scopes, enabling them to hit targets at a distance of 900yd. Personnel detectors, or 'people sniffers', carried in helicopters sensed microscopic particles in the air and were supposed to detect even the ammonia excretions from men on the ground.

Much trouble was taken by the Americans to conceal their own movements. Special aircraft with muffled engines were used for reconnaissance. Low-flying helicopters laid smoke-screens and smoke-generators were operated on the ground to cover troop movements. Decoy gun positions were constructed to attract enemy fire.

Yet the deployment of the sophisticated American devices did not prevent the enemy from moving when and where they liked. Such desperate measures as cutting down the jungle on either side of their supply trails and the use of herbicides to remove vegetation affording cover to guerrillas and mobile columns proved in the long run to be ineffective. Concealment and deception were undoubtedly prime factors in the success of the communists, who were continually under aerial surveillance from helicopters and attacks from various forms of aircraft.

Not only in 'minor' wars like Vietnam or the short-term Middle East conflicts, but in the event of a continental war fought between the NATO and Warsaw Pact powers with conventional weapons, camouflage would be used to the full. Moreover, the strategy of 'flexible response' currently in operation and the possibility of losing local air superiority provide motives for paying close attention to camouflage. In any case the lethality of modern weapons is such that no one on the modern battlefield is likely to ignore the practice of concealment. Modern techniques have also made possible greater mobility at night.

In response to the improved detection methods just described, and to precision-guided missiles homing on heat emissions, scientists have been busy experimenting with new camouflage techniques in defence-establishment laboratories.[4] The scientist has taken the place of the engineer and artist because of his knowledge of materials. Paint and nets continue to be the basis of camouflage, but they have to be effective throughout the electro-magnetic spectrum—ultra-violet, infra-red and micro-wave bands.

Paints able to match chlorophyll afford protection against near-infra-red detection devices. Traditional disruptive painting may also be useful as the picture presented is in monochrome, which makes it more difficult to detect colour differences. Paints are ineffective against heat emissions, the principal sources of thermal infra-red signals. In this case structural measures, such as shielding or special nets, are required.

Nets, making use of the latest materials, are designed to merge into the backgrounds against which they will be used. They are predominantly white (for snow), green (vegetation), or tan (desert or rock). If the smaller areas of red and brown earth are included, this will account for about 98 per cent of the earth's surface. In Western Europe fighting would take place in woodland, heath and over cultivated fields. Nets are therefore given light-reflecting chlorophyll properties similar to the foliage against which they are disposed. As snow has a very high ultra-violet reflectance, nets must have a similar response and such equipment as skis and snow-traversing vehicles have to be covered with paint of a high ultra-violet reflection value. Nets which are a combination of green and white have been designed for use against a partially snow-covered background.

Scientific study of texture, begun by Littlefield at Leamington,[5] shows how little gloss there is in nature. (When examined closely leaves appear shiny, but foliage seen from a little distance has no trace of gloss because reflection occurs in different directions.) Grooved texture, on the other hand, is present in all natural backgrounds—soil, sand, grass and trees, for instance. Based on this principle, a new camouflage net has been designed by incising a shiny coated fabric with a number of short, curved knives and then pulling it back, giving it a three dimensional effect. The result has the effect of hindering both visual and photographic identification.

Nets are still used to conceal guns and missiles. As before, they must be able to be placed and taken down rapidly and must not impede the field of fire. Umbrellas have been devised (not unlike Gen Thorne's parasols) which may be fixed to the weapon or stuck in the ground as cover against air reconnaissance. Ordinary nets are useless against radar waves, but nets made of PVC combined with a special material may conceal tanks and aircraft when immobile. They enable the radar image of the object and the net to merge into that of the surrounding background.

Although laser detection devices give warning that vehicles are being irradiated by laser beams, radiation from lasers may be scattered by nets causing a blurred picture on the observer's screen.

Helicopters are now indispensable on the battlefield, but are easily detectable by their noise and when resting on the ground by the rotor blades which cast revealing shadows. Non-reflective paint will reduce the body's visibility and, to some extent, the shine from motionless rotor blades. Skilful use of cover when in flight is the best form of protection against radar.

Airfields are no less inconspicuous than before and decoy aircraft continue to be employed, for example, by the Egyptians in the 1967 and 1973 wars, to divert enemy reconnaissance. Ideally in war temporary bases should be used and roads adapted as runways. The speed and noise of combat aircraft renders camouflage largely superfluous, though such low-flying close-support aircraft as the Harrier are still painted with disruptive patterns.

Radar-absorbing paint will make naval vessels less visible at sea, though large-scale actions between surface fleets are unlikely in the future. Coastal forces will continue to make use of netting when sheltering alongside steep cliffs or a rocky coastline.

Too much stress should not be laid on sophisticated equipment. The mass of information they garner must be centralised, digested and assessed, all of which takes time. The human eye (*pace* Helmholtz) is still more efficient than an electronic device, able to see and assess and take decisions instantly. Control in the battlefield cannot be exercised by automatons; it must be exercised by the commander on the spot. As a contemporary senior officer has written : 'Those who insist on commanding by radio from bunkers, playing a military form of chess, will learn that the enemy is playing to a different set of rules.'[6] Moreover, the profusion of radio communications, not to mention the wide employment of radar, will, as before, provide ample opportunities for deception and electronic countermeasures.

The possibility of nuclear warfare, not hitherto mentioned, is a threat which camouflage can do little, if anything, to counter. All that can be done is to place headquarters and command posts underground, as in the USA, while regional headquarters designed to cope with the aftermath of a nuclear attack in Britain and other countries in Europe have also been buried deep in the earth.

CONCLUSION

To prepare a sham action with sufficient thoroughness to impress
an enemy requires a considerable expenditure of time and effort
and the costs increase with the scale of the deception.

Clausewitz, *On War*

The scientific principle involved in all camouflage is to reduce as
far as possible the contrast between a target and its background
be the contrast in size, shape, movement, colour, heat emission
or radar echo.

Technical memorandum, Ministry of Defence.

The history of camouflage as an established branch of warfare is a
relatively short one and has now passed from the stage of inspired
improvision to the province of the scientist and technologist. Yet in the
literature of war it is a neglected subject; even the official histories
pay small attention to it.

Of the two types of camouflage described, static camouflage was
first practised in the siege warfare of the Western Front and twenty-
one years later in the concealment of industrial targets not only in
Britain but also in America where targets were within range of attack.
By the time radio and radar navigational and bombing aids were
sufficiently accurate not to rely on the human eye the war was well
advanced. Camouflage in the meantime had played its part, in Britain
mainly before the Battle of Britain had assured air superiority. But
failure to camouflage would have made the task of the lone bomber
attacking a vital target that much easier. In Germany inability to
control camouflage led to over-elaboration, easily spotted by photographic reconnaissance. Bombing techniques in general tended towards
saturation rather than pin-point bombing.

Leamington employed its combination of artists, scientists, architects
and other specialists with imagination. What it achieved—emergency
treatment for 560 sites, specific instructions to over 4,000 vital factories
and attention given to several thousand less important targets or land-
marks—should not obscure the important research work done and the
elimination of unnecessary camouflage which prevented the excesses
committed by the Germans.[1] Leamington's influence extended even
to Russia, visited by Glasson after the German invasion, while Ironside
gave the Americans (then camouflaging aircraft factories on their
western coast against Japanese long-range attack) the benefit of the
latest techniques employed in the Blitz.

Claims might be made for the greater success of decoys. But here bombs destined for the real target could actually be counted; how many aircrews were momentarily baffled by camouflage will never be known. Decoys nevertheless were an essential part of passive defence and fitted in admirably with German pathfinding techniques. Equally, the Germans themselves scored many successes against Bomber Command with this form of deception.

Sea-going camouflage posed problems never satisfactorily resolved. The captivating designs of dazzle-painting seem to have done little to upset U-boat commanders. Failure by the Admiralty to take camouflage seriously prompted sea-going officers to take concealment into their own hands—usually with poor results. Once put on a scientific basis, attempts to reduce visibility met with some success. But the constant changing of light and the movement of ships from one hemisphere to another made a satisfactory camouflage impractical to meet all occasions, though when a ship *was* painted appropriately it had an advantage over the enemy. Again, the camoufleurs were fighting a losing battle against the advance of radar.

In the air, camouflage, again because of changing atmospheric conditions, was hard to achieve and aircraft for the most part had to compromise between being less visible in flight and remaining unobtrusive when standing on the ground. Darkness did not provide the cloak for the night-bomber which eventually had to contend with airborne radar and radar-controlled guns and searchlights.

Only on the ground did camouflage have a chance of continuously providing cover against both air and ground observers—though air superiority caused it to be neglected. It was easy in those circumstances to forget that a single reconnaissance plane could change the course of the battle if the information it brought back was correctly analysed. As with factories and ships at sea, disruptive painting of vehicles—the popular conception of camouflage—was abandoned in favour of one or two colours. Patterned designs on vehicles in the desert were soon obscured by dust and in Western Europe the painting of recognition signs made this form of camouflage illogical.

It was not then appreciated that to obtain the best results the size of the pattern should be related to the distance at which an observation will be made. In a recent study it has been noted that this limit to size is unrelated to the eye's ability to resolve segments of the field of view. 'Instead, a close relation is found to the average state of irregularities to the background pattern. Thus, an insect, crawling over rough sand, would need a sharply-defined and small-size pattern, but a man requires a pattern scaled to his surroundings.'[2] By the end of World War II the only patterned item of equipment in the British Army was the paratrooper's smock. The German Army was addicted to disruptive patterning, both for uniforms (buff, brown and green) and their armoured vehicles which were sprayed with patches of disruptive colour. But the British did not find this had any effect in reducing visibility.

Countershading, common in nature, was rarely used successfully on equipment in the field, one exception being the attempt to make a 17-pounder gun mounted on a Sherman tank resemble a 75mm gun —half the length of the former.

As the gospel of camouflage was spread by the evangelists from Farnham and equivalent establishments in the USA, percolating to the smallest formation, the specialists could apply themselves to deception. Commanders with imagination—Allenby, Wavell and Slim— appreciated its importance and transmitted their enthusiasm to their staffs. Where the soil was fertile deception could flourish. There were two triumphs, at El Alamein and the deception scheme for the Normandy landings, but deception was skilfully injected into the planning of a number of battles in Italy and Burma.

The military thinker Carl Clausewitz, author of the classic study *On War*, first published in 1832, which has influenced generations of soldiers, statesmen and intellectuals from Bismarck and Marx to contemporary strategists, commented on deception (see the epigraph of this chapter) rather coolly. He found that craft, cleverness and cunning did not figure prominently in the history of war. Linking deception with surprise, he considered that the latter was only possible in a tactical context. But the advance of military technology, particularly in communications, since Clausewitz's day has, as has been shown, greatly increased the possibilities of surprise and deception. The use of deceptive devices make it unnecessary to use 'substantial forces merely to create an illusion' as Clausewitz averred, though he shrewdly concluded that the 'weaker the forces that are at the disposal of the supreme commander, the more appealing the use of cunning becomes'.

Camouflage on the Russian Front: motor vehicles in thin wood hidden by pulling tree tops together (*Public Record Office*)

Camouflage on the Russian Front: Truck parked on a dark patch in a snowy
period of the year to make it less visible (*Public Record Office*)

But here, too, the increase in firepower has made surprise necessary,
even for forces superior in numbers, to avoid having grievous losses
inflicted during an attack.

Any history which fails to take account of the titanic struggle on the
Eastern Front between 1941 and 1945 would be lop-sided. Too little
is known of the technical history of that campaign. Important contributions to the study of optical problems were made by Russian
scientists and in the field the Red Army took camouflage very
seriously. Dummy figures were manipulated to attract enemy fire;
dummy bridges were erected near bridges which had been half
destroyed to divert attention of hostile aircraft, the ruined bridge being
selected for the actual crossing; dummy tanks attracted hundreds of
shells and bombs; special attention was paid to the concealment of
snipers and to camouflage in snow.

Camouflage in both world wars was essentially a matter of individual effort and prominence has inevitably been given in these pages
to pioneers such as Solomon, Palmer, Glasson, Turner, Schuil and
Buckley. Inevitably no mention has been made of many men of distinction in their own unwarlike professions, some eccentric, many
light-hearted, but all enthusiastic and contributing to what others
thought was at best an esoteric pursuit and at worst a waste of time.

With the domination of the battlefield by technology, camouflage
may still, should the occasion arise, save life and provide the means
for surprise by denying information to the enemy about dispositions
and activities. Even outside the military sphere some of the methods
employed might have relevance. It is perhaps not too frivolous to
suggest, when society is belatedly becoming aware of the need to
preserve its environment, that architects and planners in developing
their designs could benefit by mastering the principles of camouflage.

SELECT BIBLIOGRAPHY

The literature on camouflage and deception is scarce and as far as is known this book is the first attempt at a general history. The following may be found helpful. Place of publication is London unless otherwise stated.

Addison, Col G. H., *The Work of the Royal Engineers in the European War, 1914–18*, 1926. Contains an account of camouflage on the Western Front, including the pioneer work by the French.

Barkas, G., *The Camouflage Story*, 1952. Good on the Western Desert, but does not go beyond El Alamein.

Breckenridge, R. P., *Modern Camouflage. The New Science of Protective Concealment*, New York, 1942.

Chesney, Lt-Col C. H. R., *The Art of Camouflage*, 1941. Chesney was in charge of the camouflage factory at Amiens in World War I and he gives valuable insight on the Western Front. Four chapters by J. Huddlestone deal with industrial camouflage.

Cott, H., *Adaptive Coloration in Animals*, 1940. Many references to military camouflage by the author, a friend of Sir John Graham Kerr, another eminent zoologist interested in military and naval camouflage.

Maskelyne, J., *Magic—Top Secret*, c1948. An entertaining account of the well-known conjuror's experiences in camouflage.

Scott, P., *The Eye of the Wind*, 1961. His autobiography, which gives an account of the genesis of the 'Western Approaches' scheme.

Solomon, S. J., *Strategic Camouflage*, 1920. Solomon's theory about German camouflage on the Western Front was not shared by the Army.

Thayer, Abbott H., *Concealing Coloration in the Animal Kingdom*, 1909. Primarily an artist, Thayer was a pioneer in animal camouflage, which led him to write on military camouflage.

Trevelyan, J., *Indigo Days*, 1957. Contains a lively account of camouflage in England in World War II and a visit to the Middle East in 1942.

Wilkinson, N., *A Brush with Life*, 1969. Interesting chapters on both world wars by the pioneer of dazzle-painting.

Witteman, K. F., *Industrial Camouflage*, New York, 1942. Gives a brief account of American Army camouflage on the Western Front.

REFERENCES

NOTE

Many of the sources for this book will be found in the Public Record Office. Documents relating to static camouflage in World War II are contained in the files of the Home Office and the Ministry of Home Security (HO series). More material on the camouflage of airfields and the operation of decoys will be found in the Air Ministry files (Air series). The scientific aspects of sea-going camouflage in 1939–45 will also be found in the HO series, though other aspects are contained in the Admiralty ADM series. The latter contains papers on decoys and dazzle-painting in World War I. Army camouflage and deception are covered by the War Office files (WO series). The story of reducing the visibility of aircraft in flight may be traced in the Ministry of Supply AVIA series.

INTRODUCTION

1 Cott, H., *Adaptive Coloration in Animals*, 1940, *passim*; Frisch, Otto von, *Animal Camouflage*, 1973; Friedmann, H., *The Natural History Background of Camouflage*, Smithsonian Instn, 1942.
2 *Encyclopaedia Brit.*, 1922 edn, 'Camouflage' (F. J. C. Wyatt).
3 Cadell, Sir P., *'Beginnings of Khaki'*, *Jnl of Soc for Army Hist Res*, vol **XXXI**, 1953.
4 Fuller, Maj-Gen J. F. C., *The Conduct of War*, 1962, p140.
5 Ministry of Defence Cent Library, Hist Mem. 142.
6 Kerr, Prof G., 'Camouflage of Ships and the Underlying Scientific Principles', *Jnl NE Coast Instn of Engnrs & Shipbuilders*, July 1919.
7 Luckiesh, M., 'Aeroplane Visibility', *Jnl of the Franklin Inst*, Mar–Apr 1919; 'The Principles of Camouflage', *Trans Illuminating Engng Soc*, vol 14, 1919.
8 'War Paint', *Flight*, 29 Apr 1937.

CHAPTER 1

1 Fuller, Maj-Gen J. F. C., op cit, p161.
2 *Encyclopaedia Brit.*, 1922 edn, 'Camouflage'.
3 Addison, Col G. H., *The Work of the RE in the European War 1914–18*, Vol Misc, Sect B, 'Camouflage'.
4 Phillips, Olga S., *Solomon J. Solomon. A Memoir of Peace and War*, Ch 6, ND; Neve, C., *Leon Underwood*, 1974.
5 PRO/WO95/120.

6 Swinton, Maj-Gen Sir E., *Eye Witness*, 1932.
7 Phillips, Olga S., op cit.
8 PRO/WO95/120; Chesney, Lt-Col C. H. R., *The Art of Camouflage*, 1941.
9 Phillips, Olga S., op cit.
10 PRO/WO95/127.
11 Solomon, S. J., *Strategic Camouflage*, 1920, *passim*.
12 PRO/WO95/127.
13 Liddell Hart, B. H., *Thoughts on War*, 1944, p206.
14 Wavell, Gen Sir A., *Allenby*, 1940, Chs 8–10.
15 PRO/WO187/1.

CHAPTER 2

1 PRO/ADM131/85.
2 Campbell, Capt G., RN, *My Mystery Ships*, 1928, *passim*.
3 Newbolt, Sir H., *Naval Operations*, vol V, 1931.
4 Steele, Lt G. C., RN, 'Decoy as a Weapon in Naval Warfare', *RUSI Jnl*, Feb 1923.
5 Kerr, J. G., correspondence on camouflage, 1914–18, Univ of Glasgow Archives; Admiralty Mem 'The Camouflage of Ships at Sea', CB 3098 (45).
6 PRO/ADM1/8485/77.
7 PRO/ADM1/8482/50.
8 Wilkinson, N., *A Brush with Life*, 1969; 'Dazzle-Painting of Ships', *Engng*, vol CVII, 8 Aug 1919.
9 Buskirk, Lt H. Van, USN, 'Camouflage', *Illum Engng Soc* (USA), vol 14, 1919.
10 PRO/ADM1/8533/215; PRO/MT25/16.
11 Gibson, R. H. and Prendergast, M., *German Submarine Warfare*, 1931.

CHAPTER 3

1 PRO/CAB16/170.
2 PRO/HO186/390.
3 Carline, R., letter to author, 18 Aug 1978.
4 PRO/HO186/1648.
5 PRO/HO191/3; PRO/HO186/1987.
6 PRO/HO196/31.
7 PRO/HO186/668.
8 Trevelyan, J., *Indigo Days*, 1957, pp112–14.
9 Kerr, J. G., correspondence on camouflage, Univ of Glasgow Archives, 1939–42.
10 Merton, Prof T. R., letter in *Nature*, 28 Sept 1940.
11 PRO/HO186/12; PRO/HO186/171; PRO/HO186/668.
12 PRO/HO186/1985; PRO/HO186/1989.

13   PRO/HO186/1986.
14   PRO/HO217/10.
15   PRO/HO186/1342.
16   PRO/HO191/3.

CHAPTER 4

1   PRO/HO186/1342.
2   PRO/HO186/972.
3   PRO/AVIA46/148 (narrative written by R. Carline for MAP).
4   PRO/HO186/1331.
5   Carline, R., letter to author, 18 Aug 1978.
6   Wilkinson, N., op cit; PRO/AIR20/5188.
7   PRO/HO186/1981; PRO/HO216/1.
8   PRO/AIR20/5188.
9   PRO/HO186/1332; PRO/HO186/170.
10   PRO/HO186/1334.
11   PRO/HO217/4.
12   PRO/HO191/3; PRO/HO217/7.
13   PRO/HO186/669; PRO/HO195/27; PRO/HO186/1897.
14   PRO/HO186/1342.
15   PRO/AIR20/5188; PRO/HO186/391; PRO/AIR20/4353.
16   PRO/AIR20/4354; PRO/HO186/1985.
17   PRO
18   *United States Strategic Bombing Survey*, vol V, 1945.
19   PRO/HO186/1988.

CHAPTER 5

1   PRO/AVIA13/603.
2   Beddington, Lt-Col F., letter to author, 20 June 1978.
3   PRO/WO167/48.
4   Trevelyan, J., op cit, pp116–20; information from André Bicât and Reg Lander, 1978.
5   Imp War Mus, Ashley Havinden Colln.
6   PRO/AVIA15/843.
7   Trevelyan, J., op cit, p178.
8   PRO/WO32/10172.
9   PRO/WO199/2412.
10   PRO/WO199/1314;   PRO/WO199/1332;   PRO/WO199/1629.
11   Information supplied by Lt-Col E. G. Boxshall.
12   PRO/WO199/2544.
13   PRO/WO199/1327; PRO/WO199/1328.
14   Imp War Mus, Ashley Havinden Colln.

CHAPTER 6

1   Barkas, G., *The Camouflage Story*, 1952, *passim*.
2   Imp War Mus, Ashley Havinden Colln.
3   PRO/WO169/5409.
4   PRO/WO201/2021.
5   PRO/WO201/2033.
6   Imp War Mus, Ashley Havinden Colln.
7   PRO/ADM1/171814.
8   PRO/ADM1/171814.
9   PRO/WO170/1853; PRO/WO170/5199.
10 PRO/WO170/1854; PRO/WO170/5120.
11 PRO/WO204/7996.
12 PRO/WO201/2025.
13 PRO/WO204/7993.
14 PRO/WO204/8005.
15 André Bicât, interviewed by author, 27 July 1978.
16 PRO/WO203/5742; PRO/WO203/3313.
17 PRO/WO203/640.
18 PRO/WO172/7192.
19 PRO/WO203/3436; PRO/AVIA22/2228.
20 Slim, Field Marshal Sir W., *Defeat into Victory*, 1956, p395.
21 Dod, Karl C., *Corps of Engineers. The War against Japan*, OCMH, Washington, 1966.

CHAPTER 7

1   PRO/HO186/395.
2   Pawle, G., *The Secret War, 1939–45*, 1956, pp51–2.
3   PRO/ADM199/1096.
4   PRO/ADM1/11171.
5   Scott, P., *The Eye of the Wind*, Ch 14, 1961.
6   PRO/HO217/7.
7   PRO/ADM199/1096.
8   PRO/HO196/31.
9   Hodges, P., *Royal Navy Warship Camouflage*, 1973.
10 PRO/HO191/2.
11 PRO/ADM116/5237.
12 Ibid.
13 PRO/ADM1/15214.
14 PRO/ADM1/17606.
15 PRO/ADM212/132.
16 PRO/ADM1/17004.
17 Admiralty Mem, 'The Camouflage of Ships at Sea', CB 3098 (45); Goodden, R. Y., letter to author, 10 Sept 1978.
18 PRO/ADM116/5237.
19 Ibid.

20 Ibid.
21 PRO/ADM1/13676.
22 Muggenthaler, A. K., *German Raiders of World War II*, 1978, *passim*.
23 PRO/AVIA13/566.
24 PRO/AVIA13/567; PRO/AVIA13/568.
25 PRO/AVIA13/573; PRO/AVIA13/610.
26 Waddington, C. H., *Operational Research in World War II*, 1973; PRO/AVIA13/1153.
27 PRO/AVIA13/1403.
28 PRO/AVIA13/1403; PRO/AVIA15/1425; Jones, E. C., letter to author, 25 Sept 1978.
29 PRO/AVIA13/615.
30 PRO/AIR14/1892; PRO/AVIA13/1084.
31 Royal Soc Memoirs of Fellows, 'T. R. Merton', vol 16, 1970.
32 PRO/AVIA13/613.
33 PRO/AIR14/1892.
34 PRO/AVIA15/1442.
35 PRO/AVIA15/2630.
36 PRO/AVIA15/1084.

CHAPTER 8

1 Greenwood, T., 'Reconnaissance, Surveillance and Arms Control', *Adelphi Paper No 88*, Int Inst of Strategic Studies, 1972.
2 'Modern Camouflage Techniques from Sweden—The Barracuda System', *Int Defence Rev*, vol 7, Apr 1974.
3 Hay, Lt-Gen John H., *Vietnam Studies. Tactical and Material Innovations*, Dept for Army, Washington, 1974.
4 Overton, T. K., 'Camouflage Colours', *Jnl of the Soc of Dyers & Colourists*, vol 85, Apr 1969, pp152–5.
5 Stores and Clothing Research and Development Establishment, Min of Defence, tech memoranda.
6 Farrar-Hockley, A., 'The Scope and Direction of New Conventional Weapons Technology', *Adelphi Paper No 144*, Int Inst of Strategic Studies, 1978.

CONCLUSION

1 O'Brien, T. H., *Civil Defence* (British Official Histories—Civil Series), 1955.
2 Overton, T. K., op cit.

ACKNOWLEDGEMENTS

I would like to thank the following for their help, either in reading draft chapters, giving me the benefit of their memories of camouflage, or information about the current practice of camouflage: Lt-Col F. Beddington, Mr André Bicât, Mr G. Earwicker, Prof Richard Guyatt, Mr Christopher Ironside, Mr G. Johansson of Barracudaverken AB, Dr E. C. Jones, Mr Reg Lander, Mr Martin Muncaster, son of Claude Muncaster, and author of a memoir *The Wind in the Oak* with an interesting chapter on naval camouflage, Mr Terry Overton of the Ministry of Defence, Mr Alan Raven, Mr Brian Robb, Mr Sydney Robinson, Mr Humphrey Spender, Mr B. A. Stokes of Bridport-Gundry Ltd, Mr Brian Thomas and Mr Julian Trevelyan.

I am particularly grateful to Lt-Col E. G. Boxshall, Mr Richard Carline and Professors Robert Goodden and David Pye for their written contributions, heavily drawn on for Chapters 3, 5 and 7 respectively.

My thanks are also due to the staffs of the following institutions: the Archives, University of Glasgow for giving me access to the papers of Sir John Graham Kerr, the Library of the Institution of Mechanical Engineers, the Air Historical Branch and the Naval Historical Section of the Ministry of Defence, Mr Potts and the Central Library of the Ministry of Defence, the Science Museum Library, the Imperial War Museum and the Public Record Office, from which I gathered most of the material on camouflage during the two world wars.

Finally, I must thank the following for permission to use illustrations: the Public Record Office for photographs and drawings which are Crown Copyright; the Imperial War Museum for photographs and drawings; the remainder were kindly supplied by friends to whom thanks are also due.

INDEX